Acknowledgments

Dr. L. C. Chadwick and Professor F. W. Dean were authors of earlier editions of this book, and their significant contributions are acknowledged, including Dr. Chadwick's original keys to plant identification. Both Chadwick and Dean are deceased and have not been involved with the project for more than 20 years, thus their names were omitted as authors. Faculty currently involved with this project have been continued as authors.

Mrs. Mary Murnieks, School of Natural Resources, typed the entire manuscript as the text was not in electronic format.

Acknowledgment is made to the United States Department of Agriculture and the United States Forest Service in cooperation with various states in preparing and publishing similar tree guides for use with portions of the text. These states include Tennessee, North Carolina, Virginia, Maryland, Illinois, and Oklahoma. Acknowledgment is also made to the American Tree Association, Washington, D. C., for valuable material from its book, *Common Trees of Ohio*, by Joseph S. Illick.

Additional acknowledgment is given to The Ohio State University's School of Natural Resources and Ohio Agricultural Research and Development Center, who loaned cuts and photographs for the manual. These cuts were made from the original drawings by Mrs. A. E. Hoyle of the United States Forest Service. Professor J. S. Illick of the New York State College of Forestry at Syracuse University, N.Y., kindly loaned a number of zinc etchings. Other artistic renditions were made by John Nagy, Elaine Shay, and Alison Reader. A complete listing of renditions by each artist can be found under their names in the index of this book.

The classification and terminology were adapted from a *Manual of Cultivated Trees and Shrubs*, by Alfred Rehder. This text was also used as a general reference in describing many species and varieties. Nomenclature is according to the *International Code of Nomenclature*, 1958, with few exceptions.

Distribution references of species in the state were taken from personal observations and from *The Woody Plants of Ohio*, by E. Lucy Braun, 1961 edition. Dr. Braun's book is one of several contributions to a continuing project to develop *The Vascular Flora of Ohio*.

Ohio Trees

Ohio is part of the great central-hardwood-forest region. Geographically, it lies near the north-central portion of this extensive region that extends northward to Michigan and Wisconsin, eastward to the Atlantic coast, southward to the pine areas of Georgia, Arkansas, and Texas, and westward to the Great Plains and prairie states. A great many trees representative of other forest regions extend into Ohio. For example, in northeastern Ohio the white pine, hemlock, yellow birch, beech, and sugar maple grow native. These trees are typical of northern forest areas. In southeastern Ohio the shortleaf, pitch, and scrub pines are more typical of the southern forest regions. Hardwoods of the southern forest region include the blackjack oak, Spanish oak, sourwood, and bigleaf magnolia that have advanced into the state from the lower Allegheny and Appalachian areas. In southeastern Ohio many trees are limited in their distribution and are entirely confined to southern Ohio.

The state forest park areas of Hocking and Fairfield counties contain many examples of the overlapping and blending of northern and southern species. The hemlock, Canadian yew, and black birch are found as remnants of a northern-type forest surrounded by a southern-climate forest of the oak, hickory, chestnut-type, associated with rare species from the south such as umbrella magnolia, shortleaf pine, rhododendron, sourwood, fringetree, and aralia, or Hercules' club.

The greater portion of Ohio's land area was once covered with a dense, virgin forest. Of the almost 26.1 million acres of land, approximately 25 million acres were covered with forests. By 1940, this huge forest had been reduced to about 1.6 million acres, or about 10 percent of the total land area. Clearing for agricultural purposes was the principal reason for the clearings. Over the last 50 years, Ohio has added to its woodlands. By 1996, Ohio had 7.9 million forested acres and was 30 percent wooded.

Breaks in the original forest area existed in the western sections of the state where prairie openings or patches existed and in the wetlands along the Lake Erie shore. Prairie openings were typical of Indiana, Illinois, and Iowa and were dominated by tall prairie grasses. Associated with these openings or patches were scattered trees of open-forest growth, characterized by a bur oak-hickory type that is commonly distributed in Madison, Champaign, Fayette, Greene, and Clark counties today. There were, however, no extensive areas comparable to the vast prairie openings of the middle western states.

The forests of Ohio contain a wealth of native tree species. At least 120 species of trees are native to the state, not including the small trees such as hawthorns that would add approximately 30 more species or varieties to the list. Of the 120 species of native trees, 14 species belong to the oaks, six to the hickories, six to the ash, and seven to the maple group. In addition, 15 species of willow have been identified in the state, although only three are of commercial importance.

Southeastern Ohio probably has the greatest number and type of native trees. In a forest survey made by the Ohio Department of Natural Resources, Division of Forestry, a complete checklist was made of all native trees in 10 southeastern counties. A total of 87 species of native forest trees were found growing in the 10-county area. Of the 87 species, 13 were oaks,

3

including two extremely rare oaks to Ohio. The blackjack oak and the Spanish oak also were discovered. Of the total number of trees growing in the surveyed areas, 45 of the 87 species were of commercial importance for saw logs, lumber, pulpwood, and post purposes.

The Value of Trees

All trees have their own purposes. Some are valued for the production of lumber, while others are used as beautiful shade trees because of their form and habit of growth. Other trees are used for urban uses. These same trees afford shelter, food, and protection to both bird and animal life, whether planted around homes or growing in fields and forests. They protect soils from erosion, conserve moisture, protect water quality, and modify both soil and air temperature extremes during the summer and winter months. Trees reduce energy use by filtering winds, blocking summer sun, and allowing the passage of winter sunlight. Recently, there has been evidence showing the presence of vegetation, especially trees in urban areas, encourages positive interactions among people and is associated with lower crime rates.

Several of our native forest trees serve dual purposes. They are valued for both their timber and their aesthetic qualities. The green ash and red oak are fine examples of trees suitable for timber as well as for shade and street planting.

Trees for Lumber Purposes

The trees most important for lumber usage are white oak, black walnut, tulip tree, red oak, white ash, sugar maple, basswood, American elm, slippery elm, wild black cherry, bur oak, and swamp white oak.

Trees for Shade and Ornamental Purposes

The native Ohio trees best adapted for shade and ornamental purposes include sugar maple, red oak, bur oak, pin oak, black tupelo, sweet gum, flowering dogwood, red maple, redbud, honeylocust, white pine, and Washington hawthorn.

A list of exotic trees (not native to Ohio) that have been planted extensively for shade and ornamental purposes includes: Norway maple, London planetree, little-leaf linden, Austrian pine, Scotch pine, and Colorado blue spruce.

Trees for Windbreaks and Reforestation

Norway spruce, Austrian pine, red pine, white pine, and Eastern arborvitae are used extensively for windbreak plantings. Conifers assist with reforestation. Both the white pine and the Austrian pine have been planted around farmsteads.

Identifying Trees

In addition to the keys and description of trees, frequent visits to woodland areas are necessary to become thoroughly acquainted with our native trees and shrubs. Only with experience in the field observing the various types and forms, combined with the technical knowledge of trees, can one master the complete identification of trees. (See individual keys accompanying each genus.)

Most of our cities and towns have parks and cemeteries where a great variety of trees are found, including native, rare, and exotic types. A good example is the Spring Grove Cemetery in Cincinnati that contains a wealth of native trees and a variety of fine specimens of ornamental trees introduced from other regions of the world (exotics).

The metropolitan park areas of major cities and towns, where a wide assortment of trees can be found, are open to the public for hikes and excursions. Also, many species, varieties, and cultivars of trees and other woody plants are growing in Ohio's arboretums, such as the Mt. Airy Forest Arboretum and the Stanley M. Rowe Arboretum in Cincinnati, the Cox Arboretum in Dayton, Crosby Gardens in Toledo, Dawes Arboretum in Newark, Holden Arboretum in Mentor, and the Secrest Arboretum at The Ohio State University's Ohio Agricultural Research and Development Center in Wooster. All of these arboreta are open to the public. Since the plants in arboreta are usually well-labeled, they afford individuals, schools, and organizations a source of named plants for observation and study.

Some Historic Trees of Ohio

Of all the trees in Ohio identified with history, the Logan Elm is the best known and perhaps the most beautiful. This tree was 70 feet tall and had a 7-foot-diameter trunk (measured 6 feet above the ground). The limb spread was 148 feet across. The original site of this tree is now the Logan Elm State Park and is located about 6 miles south of Circleville in Pickaway County.

The Rathborne Elm near Marietta was thought to be the largest elm in the world. At 4½ feet above the ground, the trunk diameter was 8⅓ feet. The crown spread was 132 feet (see below). The Logan and Rathborne Elms are now dead.

Table 1.
Some Ohio champion "Big Trees" were compiled from records of the Ohio Forestry Association, 1997. Plants are arranged alphabetically by common name.

Common Name	Scientific Name	Trunk Diameter (inches)	Height (feet)	Spread (feet)
American elm	Ulmus americana	85	118	107
American sycamore	Platanus occidentalis	185	129	105
Common honeylocust	Gleditsia triacanthos	74	76	74
Chinquapin oak	Quercus muehlenbergii	84	72	66
Flowering dogwood	Cornus florida	21	26	27
Ohio buckeye	Aesculus glabra	52	82	67
Osage-orange	Maclura pomifera	106	72	86
Red oak	Quercus rubra	103	106	84
White ash	Fraxinus americana	80	115	90
White pine	Pinus strobus	33	152	46

Beneath the shade of the Oberlin elms on the campus of Oberlin College, the first log cabin in that community was built. This cabin was the beginning of the college. Oberlin was the first college to unconditionally admit women.

A magnificent hemlock at Old Man's Cave State Park, Logan, has a height of 149 feet and a trunk diameter of 40 inches, 4½ feet above the ground. Many of the trees in the hollows of Old Man's Cave State Park are thought to be part of the original forest.

An early welcome sign for Ohio visitors coming up the Ohio River was a common bald-cypress on the estate of Dr. John A. Warder in North Bend, Ohio. Because of its perfect shape and size, the tree was used as a sighting point by riverboat pilots to negotiate the Great North Bend. Today the site is a subdivision called Aston Oaks, and plans call for the home, the bald-cypress, and two of Ohio's champion trees to be preserved for their historical significance. Dr. Warder was a charter member of the American Forestry Association, host for the AFA's first meeting in Cincinnati, and an early advocate for conservation in the United States.

Key to Deciduous and Evergreen Trees of Ohio

It is the aim of the authors to encourage familiarity and increase the general knowledge of the public to trees native to state of Ohio. In addition to native trees, a few exotic trees that are thoroughly established in the state are included in this book.

While this key is to be used primarily as a foliage key, many twig and bud characteristics are given to enable the book's use during the dormant period. In preparing this key, Rehder's *Manual of Cultivated Trees and Shrubs*, 1940, was used freely. The personal experience of the authors in teaching plant identification, or dendrology, identified other characteristics used in naming plants. With few exceptions, the nomenclature follows *Hortus Third*, 1976.

The structural features of branches, twigs, buds, and leaves are shown in this key.

Leaf Margins

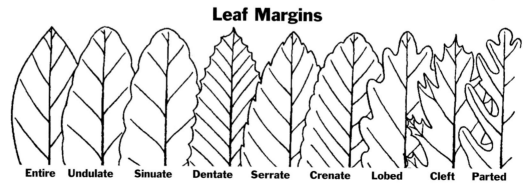

Entire   Undulate   Sinuate   Dentate   Serrate   Crenate   Lobed   Cleft   Parted

Leaf Forms

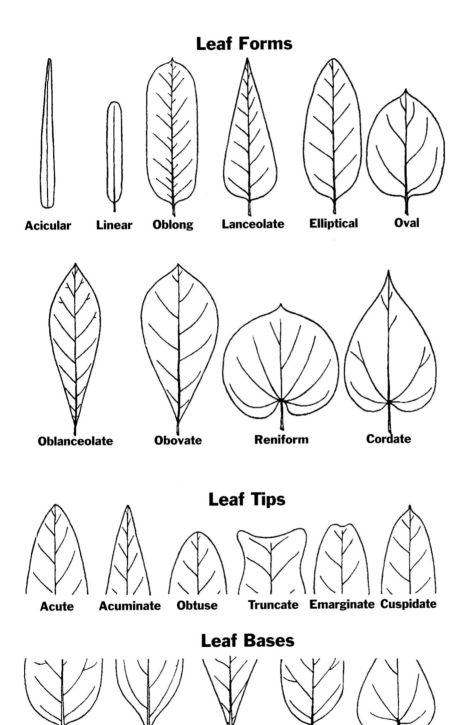

Acicular Linear Oblong Lanceolate Elliptical Oval

Oblanceolate Obovate Reniform Cordate

Leaf Tips

Acute Acuminate Obtuse Truncate Emarginate Cuspidate

Leaf Bases

Obtuse Acute Cuneate Oblique Cordate

7

Leaf Arrangement

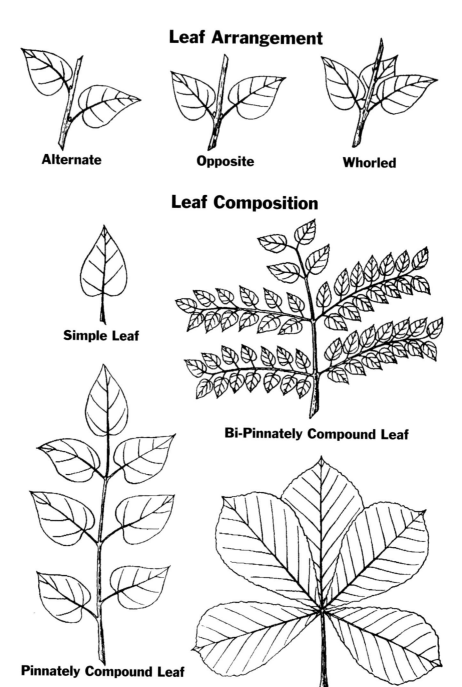

Alternate   **Opposite**   **Whorled**

Leaf Composition

Simple Leaf

Bi-Pinnately Compound Leaf

Pinnately Compound Leaf

Palmately Compound Leaf

General

Plants can be divided into two classes: (A) those with *evergreen* leaves that usually last more than a single year, and (B) those with *deciduous* leaves that are shed annually. The evergreen class can be further subdivided into three groups: 1) leaves borne in clusters or bundles as found with the pines, 2) those with leaves opposite as found with the arborvitaes and junipers (often the individual leaves are very small and close observation is necessary to determine the arrangement), and 3) leaves alternating or scattered on the twigs as found with the spruces, hemlocks, and firs.

Deciduous plants can be divided into two groups: 1) those with leaves, leaf scars, or buds opposite (two) or in whorls (three or more leaves at a single point on the stem) and 2) those with leaves, leaf scars, or buds alternating along the stem.

Each group can be divided into four subgroups: a) leaves compound, those composed of two or more similar parts or leaflets (if these parts radiate from a single point, they are termed palmately compound; if they originate from different points along a leaf stem, they are termed pinnately compound), b) leaves lobed, c) leaves toothed, and d) leaves entire. This method of grouping is used in the key starting on page 13.

Branches and Twigs

Branches and twigs are used extensively as identification points. Normally, plants have a *monopodial* branching habit, where the end bud continually takes the lead. In a few plants, such as the flowering dogwood, pagoda dogwood, and sassafras, the branching habit is termed *sympodial*. Sympodial branching is where the side bud takes the lead and the branches seemingly form in horizontal tiers.

The *pith character* is useful for identification purposes. Normally if a stem is cut in longitudinal sections, the pith appears to be continuous and of a uniform structure throughout. In some plants, such as *Nyssa sylvatica* or blackgum, the pith is interrupted at frequent intervals by partitions of firmer and darker tissue. Pith of this type is referred to as *diaphragmed*. In other plants, such as the black walnut, the parts of the pith between these firmer partitions have disappeared and have become hollow except for the partitions. This type of pith is referred to as *chambered*. Finally, in some shrubs the pith is entirely absent and is referred to as *hollow*.

Thorns are considered to be modified branches. Spines are considered to be modified stipules, or outgrowths of the cortical tissues of the stem. Lenticels, or breathing pores, appear as warty dots or patches on the surface of the stem and frequently aid in identification. Bark characteristics, twig color, and the presence or absence of hairs are other characteristics used to distinguish between twigs of different trees.

Buds

The more bud characters are used, the more useful the key becomes. Its use extends into the winter months when the leaves are no longer present on deciduous plants. However, if the key was based on bud and twig characteristics alone, it would eliminate the possibility of dividing the plants into the several groups mentioned at the beginning of this section. In most cases, the bud characters used in this key can be determined with the naked eye. However, a hand lens will always help in identification. Bud characteristics are difficult to use from late spring to early fall when rapid growth occurs and foliage is shading twigs and retarding color development.

Buds occupy a lateral or terminal position on the stem. The lateral or axillary buds are those that develop in the leaf axis, or directly above the leaf scar. The terminal bud is formed on the end of the twig and denotes the end of the present year's growth. Often a number of buds develop at each node. These accessory, or collateral, buds are often a plump flower bud on either side of the leaf bud. Sometimes there are one or more buds above the normal lateral bud. This type of bud is known as a *superposed* bud.

Occasionally, plants have what appear to be terminal buds when really they are not. This condition is brought about when the end of the twig dies back and sloughs off to the nearest lateral bud, leaving a small stub that may only be visible using a hand lens. When a bud occurs in this position, it is termed a *pseudo-terminal* bud. This pseudo-terminal bud, or lateral bud, can be determined by the leaf scar directly below it. A true terminal bud has no leaf scar.

Buds are immature branches, miniature leaves, or flowers, usually with a protective covering. With a few plants, no covering is provided, and the miniature leaves are visible. This type of bud is known as a *foliate* (naked) bud. Buds are protected by scales of varying numbers. If the scales meet like a clam shell without any overlapping visible edges, they are termed *valvate* buds. When many overlapping scales are present, they are known as *imbricated* buds. The number of overlapping scales can vary from a few to many and can be used to distinguish between plants.

Leaves, Stipules, Leaf Scars, and Stipule Scars

A complete leaf is composed of a blade (a leaf in common parlance), a petiole (leaf stalk), and stipules (appendages at the base of the petiole).

Twig Characteristics

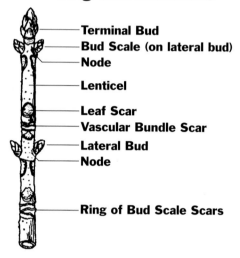

- Terminal Bud
- Bud Scale (on lateral bud)
- Node
- Lenticel
- Leaf Scar
- Vascular Bundle Scar
- Lateral Bud
- Node
- Ring of Bud Scale Scars

Leaf Characteristics

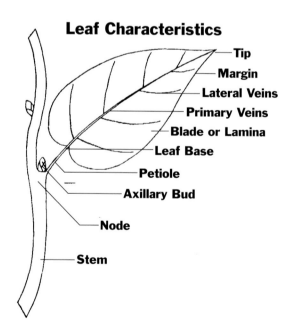

- Tip
- Margin
- Lateral Veins
- Primary Veins
- Blade or Lamina
- Leaf Base
- Petiole
- Axillary Bud
- Node
- Stem

Stipules are usually borne one on each side of the petiole. They may be persistent and stay as long as the leaf or be shed as the leaf expands and appear to be absent on the mature leaf.

The blade of the leaf varies in size, shape, and marginal features. These characteristics, together with color and extent of hairiness, are often used as identification points. Several degrees of hairiness exist. If no hairs are present, the leaf is glabrous. Other terms describing hairiness are: ciliate (margin fringed with hairs), pubescent (covered with short, soft hairs), silky (covered with adpressed, fine, and straight hairs), villous (covered with long, soft, usually curved hairs), tomentose (densely woolly), tomentum (dense covering of matted hairs), and glaucous (covered with bluish-white or bluish-gray, waxy bloom).

Leaf tips are: acute (sharp-pointed), acuminate (tapered or long-pointed), obtuse (rounded), truncate (flat), emarginate (shallow notch at tip), and cuspidate (coming to a sharp bristle-like tip). Leaf bases are: obtuse (rounded), acute (coming to a point), cuneate (coming to a sharp point), oblique (the leaf blade intersects the midrib at different points), and cordate (heart-shaped). Leaf shapes are: elliptic (outline of an ellipse—about two times as long as wide), lanceolate (lance-shaped—about four times as long as wide), linear (long and narrow with parallel sides), oblong (about three times as long as wide with nearly parallel sides), reniform (kidney-shaped), ovate (outline like a hen's egg), obovate (inversely ovate), and acicular (needle-like). A leaflet is a part of a compound leaf. Rachis is an axis bearing leaflets or flowers. Stomata are small openings in the epidermis or surface of leaf, and leaves bearing them are said to be stomatic or stomatiferous. The petiole varies in length and shape and sometimes helps in the identification of species.

Stipules vary a great deal in size, from mere threadlike appendages to those the shape and nearly the size of a small leaf. Stipules may or may not be persistent. When they fall, they leave a stipular scar on the twigs that is closely connected with the leaf scar. Stipular scars vary greatly in size and shape from a small dot to a line that encircles the twig. Stipules or their scars may be present or absent.

When leaves fall, they leave a scar varying greatly in size and shape. These are usually consistent within the genus. On the surface of the leaf scar are small dots or lines that denote the bundle scars (part of the original sap-conducting tissues). These bundle scars vary in number and pattern and are often used as characteristics for winter identification.

Flowers and Fruits

A few terms used to describe flowers are: catkin (scaly-bracted), spike (usually of unisexual flowers), bract (modified and reduced leaf subtending a flower cluster), and peduncle (stalk of a flower cluster). Several terms used to describe fruit are: drupe (a fleshy fruit with a single seed covered with a bony, inner part), samara (a winged seed), and pod (a bean-like fruit opening on one side).

Measurements and Their Equivalents

Measurements in standard botanical works are usually given in the metric system. In this key, the figures have been roughly converted to the English system to aid the reader. Equivalents are: 1 millimeter (mm) equals approximately ⅟₂₅ of an inch, 10 millimeters equals 1 centimeter (cm); 2½ centimeters equals approximately 1 inch; 1 meter equals approximately 40 inches.

Using This Key to Identify the Tree in My Yard

Since this key is different in the method by which it is used, a few words of explanation are in order. First, one should strive to obtain normal-growing twigs for identification. Branch tips should be in high light. Observations should not be made on a single leaf or twig; study several to be sure they are uniform and characteristic of the plant.

To determine the identification of a plant, turn to the *Key to Classes, Groups, Subgroups, and Genera* on page 13. First, decide between the two classes: A) leaves evergreen or B) leaves deciduous. Since all the evergreen trees included in this key are narrow-leafed with needlelike leaves, narrow-linear, or awl-shaped, there should be no difficulty in distinguishing them from deciduous or broad-leafed plants.

Assuming that the first choice was for a deciduous plant, and using red oak as an example (*Quercus rubra*), turn to Class B, leaves deciduous. Then a decision is made between the two groups: (I) leaves opposite or whorled or (II) leaves alternate. The red oak has alternate leaves and therefore is in Group II, leaves alternate. A decision must now be made between the four subgroups: (I) leaves compound, (II) leaves lobed, (III) leaves toothed, or (IV) leaves entire. Since the leaves of the red oak are lobed, it will fall in Subgroup II.

In starting the identification in Subgroup II, notice that although there are always two or more alternatives, only one will satisfy the characteristics of the plant in question (this will also be true with the other subgroups). The first alternative is: I) lobes are entire and not regularly toothed. The second alternative is: II) lobes toothed. Since I) satisfies the characteristics of the red oak, we go to: A. buds are not clustered at the end of the twigs, or the alternative, AA. buds are clustered at the ends of the twigs. AA. satisfies the characteristics of the red oak and it keys out the genus as *Quercus*, the oaks.

For the key to the oak species, turn to page 84. Here the first order is I. leaves are lobed. The alternative is II. leaves are not lobed. It was previously determined that the leaves were lobed, so move to: A. lobes of the leaves end in bristles, or its alternative, AA. lobes are rounded and are without bristle-like points. Since A. satisfies the characteristics of the red oak, go to the next order: II. leaves elliptic to oblong is correct. On to the next order, aa. is correct for the red oak, so move on. Here, ii. is correct. Finally, you will find AA) is correct, and it keys out to *Quercus rubra*, the eastern red oak.

Key to Classes, Groups, Subgroups, and Genera

Class A. Leaves are evergreen, needlelike, narrow-linear, awl-shaped, or scalelike.
    Group I—Leaves in bundles are needlelike.

Pinus—Pine   Page 38

    Group II—Leaves opposite and awl-shaped or scalelike. Leaves are small, often overlapping, and adpressed.

        I. Leaves are sharp and harsh to the touch, especially on the main branches or older twigs. Leaves are free at the apex. Fruit is berrylike.

Juniperus—Juniper   Page 24

        II. Leaves are soft to the touch and scalelike. Most are closely adpressed to the branchlets. Fruit is a woody cone with six to 12 scales.

Thuja—Arborvitae   Page 26

    Group III—Leaves are alternate and scattered on the stem. Leaves are narrow and linear.

        I. Winter buds on normal shoots are conspicuously long-pointed, brown with many scales, and non-resinous.

Pseudotsuga—Douglas-Fir   Page 31

        II. Buds are not long-pointed.
            A. Leaves are deciduous at their base. Old twigs are not roughened by persistent leaf bases.

Abies—Fir   Page 28

           AA. Leaves are deciduous above the leaf base, leaving the twigs roughened by persistent leaf bases.
              1. Leaves are flat and arranged into two planes. White, stomatic lines are present beneath the leaf. Twigs are only slightly roughened by persistent leaf bases.

Tsuga—Hemlock   Page 32

              11. Leaves are four-sided with stomatic lines of equal numbers on all sides. Twigs are strongly roughened by persistent leaf bases.

Picea—Spruce   Page 33

13

Class B. Leaves are deciduous, mostly broad, and occasionally narrow or linear.
Group I—Leaves are opposite or whorled.
Subgroup I—Leaves are compound.
I. Leaves are palmately compound.

II. Leaves are pinnately compound.
A.   Side buds are hidden.

AA. Side buds are prominent. Bundle scars are numerous.

Subgroup II—Leaves are lobed.
I. Pith is chambered or sometimes hollow.

II. Pith is solid.

Subgroup III—Leaves are toothed.
I. Petioles are connected directly or by a line around the twig.

II. Petioles are not connected either directly or by a line around the twig.

Subgroup IV—Leaves are entire.
I. Pith is chambered or sometimes hollow.

II. Pith is solid.
A.   Leaves are long-petioled, large (4–12 inches [10–30½ cm] long), and often whorled.

14

AA. Leaves are not as above.

    I.   Bundle scars are almost in a complete circle. Side buds are globular with four to five pairs of bud scales.

                Chionanthus—Fringetree   Page 196

    II.   Bundle scars and buds are not as above. Leaves have parallel veins.

                Cornus—Dogwood   Page 182

Group II—Leaves are alternate.

  Subgroup I—Leaves are compound.

  I. Leaves are twice compound.

    A.   Twigs are spiny or thorny.

      I. Spines are unbranched, short, and stout.

             Aralia—Aralia   Page 181

      II. Thorn is simple or branched, stout, and 2-4 or more inches in length.

            Gleditsia—Honeylocust   Page 144

    AA. Twigs are not spiny or thorny.

        Gymnocladus—Kentucky Coffeetree   Page 147

  II. Leaves are once compound.

    A.   Leaflets are trifoliate.

          Ptelea—Hop Tree   Page 150

    AA. Leaflets are always more than three.

      I.   Leaflets are toothed.

        a. Stems are thorny.

          i. Plants have aromatic branches when crushed.

             Zanthoxylum—Pricklyash   Page 149

          ii. Plants are without aromatic branches when crushed.

             Gleditsia—Honeylocust   Page 144

        aa. Stems are not thorny.

          i. Stipules are present, broad, and coarsely toothed.

             Sorbus—Mountain-Ash   Page 135

15

ii. Stipules are absent.
  A)   Pith is chambered.
                     Juglans—Butternut, Walnut   Page 62

  AA) Pith is solid.
    I) Buds are naked or valvate.
      a)   Buds are naked.
                     Rhus—Sumac   Page 153

      aa) Buds are valvate.
                     Carya—Hickory   Page 64

    I I) Buds have several overlapping scales.
                     Carya —Hickory   Page 64

I I. Leaflets are entire.
  a. Stipules are absent or fall early. Side buds are visible.
    i. Buds are naked.
                     Rhus—Sumac   Page 153

    ii. Buds are scaly.
                     Ailanthus —Tree of Heaven   Page 151

  aa. Stipules are present. Side buds are usually hidden by petiole bases or
      sunken beneath leaf scars.
                     Robinia—Locust   Page 146

Subgroup II—Leaves are lobed.
  I. Lobes are entire and not regularly toothed.
    A.   Buds are not clustered at the end of the twigs.
      I . Leaves on 2-year-old twigs are borne mostly in clusters of three to five on
           spurs. Leaves are fan-shaped with parallel veins.
                     Ginkgo—Ginkgo   Page 22

      I I. Leaves on 2-year-old twigs are not borne in clusters on spurs.
        a. Stipular lines encircle the twig.
                     Liriodendron—Tuliptree   Page 120

16

AA. Twigs are not thorny, but may have stiff, short, spurs.
  I. Black glands (small, short, and threadlike) are present on midrib.

Malus—Crabapple   Page 136

  II. Black glands on the midrib are absent.
    a. Veins are straight, parallel, and running to the teeth without much branching.
      i. Outer bud scales number two to four, seldom five.
        A)   Winter catkins are present. Spur-like branches are present on 2- to 3-year-old twigs, each bearing two to three leaves. Leaves are crowded almost in a whorl.

Betula—Birch   Page 70

        AA) Winter catkins and spur-like branches are absent.
          I)   Leaves are two to three times as long as they are wide. Leaf margins are coarsely toothed and leaf tips are bristle-like.

Castanea—Chestnut   Page 81

          II) Leaves are nearly as wide as they are long. Leaf bases are usually heart-shaped or lopsided.

Tilia —Linden   Page 175

      ii. Outer bud scales number five or more.
        A)   Buds are clustered at the ends of the terminal twigs.

Quercus—Oak   Page 84

        AA) Buds are not clustered at the ends of the terminal twigs.
          I)   Buds are long-pointed with many scales. Leaves are either coarsely and singly toothed or simple with a wavy margin.

Fagus—Beech   Page 78

          II) Buds are smaller and more ovate with fewer scales. Leaves are finely and doubly toothed.
            a) Leaves are rounded or heart-shaped at the base and rarely lopsided.
              I] Bud scales are marked with fine, longitudinal lines. Leaves have each side vein forming one or two branches near the margin of the leaf.

Ostrya—Hophornbeam   Page 77

II] Bud scales are without fine, longitudinal lines. Side veins are unbranched and run straight to the teeth.

    Carpinus—Hornbeam   Page 75

 aa) Leaves are usually lopsided at the base.
     Ulmus—Elm   Page 102

aa. Veins are anastomosing, branching, and curving before reaching the margin of the leaf. (reticulate)
 i. Leaf stalk is flattened vertically.

    Populus—Poplar   Page 49

 ii. Leaf stalk is not flattened vertically but is round or nearly so.
  A) Terminal bud is sticky and usually much larger than the side buds.

    Populus—Poplar   Page 49

  AA) Terminal or pseudo-terminal bud is not sticky and usually not larger than the side buds.
   I) Twigs have a bitter, almond taste.

     Prunus—Plum, Cherry Page 139

   I I) Twigs do not have a bitter, almond taste.
    a) Terminal buds are present.
     I] Pith is diaphragmed or intermittently chambered. Leaves are prominently three-veined. Teeth are missing on lower third of the margin. Leaves are usually lopsided at the base.

      Celtis—Hackberry Page 111

     II] Pith is solid. Leaves are distinctly pinnately veined. Teeth are continued from base to tip or nearly so. Buds are long and pointed with four or five scales.

      Amelanchier—Serviceberry Page 137

19

aa) Terminal bud is absent.
   I] Sap of freshly cut twigs is milky. Leaves are some-
      times lobed.

Morus—Mulberry   Page 113

II] Sap of freshly cut twigs is not milky. Leaves are
    finely toothed or nearly entire.

Oxydendrum—Sourwood   Page 186

Subgroup IV—Leaves are entire.
  I. Leaves are narrow and evergreen-like.
    A. Leaves are spirally arranged or clustered on short, lateral spurs.

Larix—Larch   Page 36

    AA. Leaves are alternate, spreading radially, or in two-ranks. Leaves are not borne
       on spurs.

Taxodium—Bald-Cypress   Page 27

  II. Leaves are broader and not evergreen-like.
    A. Stems are thorny. Sap of freshly cut twigs is milky.

Maclura—Osage-Orange   Page 115

    AA. Stems are not thorny.
      I. Stipules or their scars completely encircle the twig.

Magnolia—Magnolia   Page 116

      II. Stipules or their scars do not encircle the twig.
        a. Twigs are aromatic when crushed or broken.
          i. Leaves are variable in shape. Leaves are lobed, mitten-shaped, or
            entire.

Sassafras—Sassafras   Page 123

          ii. Leaves are always entire.

Cotinus—Smoketree   Page 157

        aa. Twigs are not aromatic when crushed or broken.
          i. Buds are clustered at the ends of the terminal twigs.

Quercus—Oak   Page 84

ii. Buds are not clustered at the ends of the terminal twigs.
  A)   Branching is sympodial (side bud takes the lead). Leaves have parallel veins.

Cornus—Dogwood   Page 182

  AA) Branching is normal or monopodial (end bud taking the lead).
     I) Leaves are palmately veined. Leaf shape is roundish or broadly ovate with heart-shaped leaf bases.

Cercis—Redbud   Page 142

    I I) Leaves are pinnately or indistinctly veined.
      a)   Pith is diaphragmed or chambered.
        I]   Terminal bud is present.
          B.   Leaves are 2–4¾ inches (5–12 cm) long, glossy above, and somewhat bloomy beneath.

Nyssa—Tupelo   Page 179

          BB. Leaves are 6–12 inches (15–30½ cm) long. Buds have only two to three scales and are woolly brown.

Asimina—Pawpaw   Page 122

        II] Terminal bud is absent.

Diospyros—Persimmon   Page 188

      aa) Pith is solid. Leaves are usually finely toothed.

Oxydendrum—Sourwood   Page 186

Trees of Ohio

Trees are arranged by families according to their botanical sequence. Within a genus, trees are arranged alphabetically to facilitate locating a specific species.

Ginkgo — Ginkgo

Ginkgos are deciduous trees with parallel-veined, fan-shaped leaves. Leaves are lobed and alternate on young growth but borne in clusters of three to five leaves on spurs of older wood. Flowers are dioecious. Fruit is drupe-like with an ill-smelling, outer fleshy coat when fully ripe.

Key to *Ginkgo* Species

I. Leaves borne mostly in clusters of three to five on spurs. Dioecious flowers are not showy and open in May. Dusty yellow or orange fruits ripen in October on female plants.

Ginkgo biloba—Ginkgo

Description of Species

Ginkgo (Maidenhair-Tree)—*Ginkgo biloba*

This native of China is easily identified by the fan-shaped leaves and open, spirally arranged spurs on the central branches or the trunk. The lobed leaves have parallel veination and are distinctive. Leaves are borne alternately on young growth but in clusters of three to five leaves on spurs of older wood. The leaves are unlike other gymnosperms, such as the pines and spruce, which are linear. The stubby spurs are also distinctive and can be seen at a distance. Twigs are stout and stiff. The upper edge of the leaf scar is fringed and contains two bundle scars.

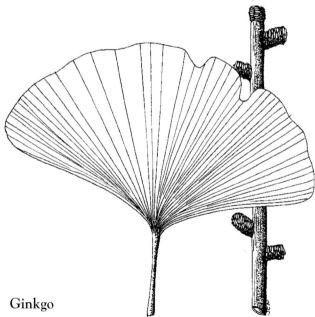

Ginkgo

22

Ginkgo (Maidenhair-Tree)

Flowers are dioecious and borne in May. The fruit matures in early fall and is yellow in color. Pulp is ill-smelling when decaying and surrounds an edible nut or seed. The roasted nut is a favorite in Oriental cooking.

Ginkgo is commonly planted in Ohio parks, gardens, and private estates. It is noted as an ornamental tree that is resistant to many insects and disease pests. Selected male cultivars are available for landscape planting, but you must be careful, as a number of cultivars introduced as males were late-flowering females. Very slow to establish, ginkgos grow rapidly after a 20-year establishment period. The habit is irregular and not dependable, even in named cultivars. The state champion in Cincinnati, Ohio, is over 80 feet high with a trunk diameter of 100 inches, and a branch spread of 104 feet.

Juniperus — Juniper

Junipers are evergreen trees or shrubs with thin, shreddy bark. Leaves are borne opposite or sometimes ternate (in threes). Leaves are short and are needle-shaped, awl-shaped or scalelike. Flowers are dioecious (male and female flowers on different plants) or monoecious (male and female flowers borne on the same plant). Flowers may be borne in the leaf axis or at the terminal end of the branch. Fruit is a cone with the fleshy scales uniting to form a berrylike structure.

Key to *Juniperus* Species

I. Leaves are sharp and harsh to the touch, especially on the main branches or older twigs. Leaves on mature plants are usually scalelike. Juvenile plants may have needle-like foliage (usually in threes), scalelike, or both. Scalelike leaves are acute or acuminate and free at the apex. Needlelike leaves most often have two white, often blended, bands on the upper surface. Bark commonly begins to shred into long strips, especially on older specimens. A typical tree is from 50–100 feet tall with red, fragrant heartwood and upright, somewhat spreading branches forming a pyramidal head. Fruit is berrylike and consists of two to 65 scales which become fleshy and unite in a berrylike structure. Fruit color is bluish or brownish-violet with a waxy bloom. Many ornamental species and varieties are found in the nursery trade.

Juniperus virginiana—Eastern Redcedar

Description of Species
Eastern Redcedar—
Juniperus virginiana

Redcedar is a very valuable tree found in all classes and conditions of soils, from swamp to dry and rich to poor. It is particularly common on poor, rocky soils where few other trees are found. It is scattered throughout the state, except in the north and northeastern portions. It is abundant on the limestone soils of southwestern Ohio, especially in Adams and Highland counties and in the western part of Pike County. This tree reaches heights of 50–100 feet with upright, somewhat spreading branches that form a pyramidal head.

Eastern Redcedar

There are two types of leaves; both are usually found on the same tree. The more typical leaf is adult foliage and is dark green, minute, and scalelike, clasping the stem in four-ranks giving the stem a square appearance. The other type of leaf usually appears on young growth or vigorous shoots and is awl-shaped. The juvenile leaves are quite sharp, pointed, spreading, and whitened. Needlelike leaves most often have two white, often blended bands on the upper surface of the foliage.

The flowers are dioecious and borne at the end of minute twigs on separate trees. Flowers may be borne in the leaf axis or at the terminal of the branch. Blooming in February or March, the male trees often assume a golden color from the small catkins, which when shaken shed clouds of yellow pollen. The ¼-inch-diameter (6 mm) fruit matures in one season and is pale blue, often with a white bloom. The berrylike fruit encloses one or two seeds in the sweet flesh, a favorite winter food for birds.

The bark is very thin and reddish-brown, peeling off in long,

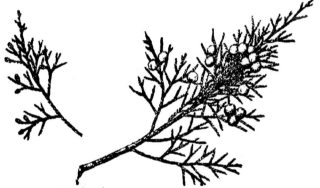

Eastern Redcedar

shred-like strips. The trunk is irregular in its growth, giving it a grooved appearance.

The heartwood is distinctly red, and the sapwood is white. The wood is sold as cedar. This color combination makes a very striking effect when finished as cedar chests, closets, and interior woodwork. The wood is aromatic, soft, strong, and of even texture. The wood scents clothing stored in cedar-lined chests. It is very durable in contact with the soil and is in great demand for posts, poles, and rustic work. Many ornamental varieties of Eastern redcedar are found in the nursery trade.

Thuja — Arborvitae

Arborvitae are evergreen trees or shrubs with scaly bark and short-spreading or ascending branches. Branchlets are flattened with scalelike leaves that are four-ranked. Flowers are monoecious and have male and female flowers in separate clusters on the same tree. Fruit is a small cone with few scales.

Key to *Thuja* Species

I. Leaves are soft to the touch and are borne opposite. Leaves are scalelike and closely adpressed to the branchlets, forming four longitudinal rows. Leaves are usually dark or bright green above, and lighter or bluish-green below. Leaves are heavier than those of *T. orientalis* and are usually glandular. It is a pyramidal tree reaching 50 feet in height. The fruit is a woody dehiscent cone with six to 12 thin scales and drops during the winter. Many ornamental varieties are available through the nursery trade.

Thuja occidentalis—Eastern Arborvitae

Description of Species
Eastern Arborvitae—*Thuja occidentalis*

The native arborvitae, also called white-cedar, is a pyramidal tree reaching 50 feet. The arborvitae is found from southern Labrador, Canada, west to Manitoba, Canada, and Minnesota, and south to North Carolina. In Ohio, this tree occurs locally in Adams, Green, and Champaign counties. It is more commonly found in the northern half of the state. The name arborvitae is French for tree of life.

The leaves are scalelike and ⅛ inch (3 mm) long. Scales closely overlap each another. Foliage is aromatic when crushed and marked with glandular dots. Leaves are arranged in pairs with each succeeding pair alternating with the next pair and forming four rows. Leaves are usually dark or bright green above and lighter or bluish-green below. Leaves are heavier or bolder than those of *T. orientalis* and are usually glandular. The cones are oblong and ½ inch (13 mm) long with six to 12 blunt-pointed, reddish-brown scales.

The trunk usually divides near the base. The bark is gray to reddish-brown and usually furrowed. Bark peels off into thin, shred-like strips.

It has been extensively planted for ornamental and windbreak purposes, particularly on lawns and in cemeteries. In nature, the tree is likely found in moist areas, floodplains, or on rocky outcrops where competition from other trees is reduced. Few other conifers tolerate moist shade. More than 50 cultivars are known. Among the most common forms are the pyramidal and the globose types. Standard and dwarf forms are available, as are color variants such as the golden-foliaged forms.

Eastern Arborvitae

26

Taxodium — Bald-Cypress

Bald-cypress is a deciduous tree with light brown, furrowed, scaly bark and upright, spreading branches. Twigs on the lower part of the shoot are deciduous and shed with the foliage. Leaves are pinnately compound, alternate, and linear with entire margins. Flowers are monoecious. Male catkins are at least 2 inches (5 cm) long and quite conspicuous during the winter months. Fruit is a golf-ball-sized cone.

Key to *Taxodium* Species

I. Leaves are soft, bright green above, and yellow or whitish-green below. Twigs near the ends of the shoots persist, while those on the lower part of the stem are deciduous and fall with the leaves.

Taxodium distichum—Common Bald-Cypress

Description of Species

Common Bald-Cypress—*Taxodium distichum*

Bald-cypress is unusual in that it is a deciduous conifer that sheds its foliage during early fall. The habit of the tree is upright with spreading branches. It is large, often 100 feet in height, with a wide, buttressed, tapering trunk. It grows in wet soils, swamps, and overflow lands of the lower Ohio and Mississippi Valley regions and from Illinois southward. When growing in water, the roots develop short, tapering trunks, protruding out of the water and known as "cypress knees."

The alternate leaves are pinnately compound. Leaflets are linear with entire margins. Foliage is soft and light green with a feathery or plume-like appearance.

Bark is light brown, furrowed, and scaly. Buds are small and inconspicuous. Twigs near the end of the shoots persist, while those on the lower part of the stem are deciduous and fall with the leaves. Flowers are monoecious. Male catkins are at least 2 inches (5 cm) long and quite conspicuous during the winter months. Fruit is a golf-ball-sized cone that matures in the fall.

Bald-cypress has been planted in Ohio as an ornamental tree and to a limited degree for timber purposes. Lumber has excellent decay resistance. Many beautiful specimens of the bald-cypress are found growing in the Cincinnati, Chillicothe, and Marietta areas and have shown value as street trees. This tree's tolerance of flooding is very high.

Common Bald-Cypress

27

Abies — Fir

Firs are evergreen trees with a pyramidal habit and spreading, whorled branches. Bark is usually smooth and thin on young trees, becoming thicker and more furrowed on older trees. Leaves are narrow and linear. Foliage is constricted above the base and is shed, leaving a relatively smooth twig. Flowers are monoecious. The fruit is a cone that is borne upright on the branches. Cone scales are shed individually with the seed, leaving a stick protruding above the branch.

Key to *Abies* Species

I. Leaves are conspicuously and uniformly bluish-green (*stomatiferous*) above and below. Foliage is 1½–2½ inches (4–6 cm) long and loosely arranged. Needles curve upward and outward. Buds are not resinous.

Abies concolor—White (Concolor) Fir

Balsam Fir

II. Leaves are not conspicuous and are uniformly bluish-green (*stomatiferous*). Stomatic areas are usually below. Slight stomatic areas often appear near the tip on the upper side of leaves of *A. balsamea.*

A. Buds are not, or only slightly, resinous. Leaves of the middle rank (leaves directly above the twig) point upward and slightly forward. Glossy, dark green needles densely cover the stem.

Abies nordmanniana—Nordmann Fir

AA. Buds are resinous. Leaves of the middle rank spread outward and somewhat upward with a few stomatic lines near the apex. One-year-old twigs are gray or reddish-gray.

Abies balsamea—Balsam Fir

Description of Species
Balsam Fir—*Abies balsamea*

The true balsam is native to the northern wooded areas of the United States and Canada. A medium size tree, the balsam fir is usually not over 75 feet in height and has a pyramidal form with spreading, whorled branches. Bark is smooth on young trees and branches. The bark is very resinous when punctured and buds are resinous as well. One-year twigs are gray or reddish-gray.

28

Needles are ½ inch (13 mm) long, flat, and spirally arranged on twigs. Foliage is soft and has a pleasant, evergreen odor. Leaves of the middle rank spread outward and somewhat upward with a few stomatic lines near the apex. Flowers are monoecious and open in May. The upright cone is less than 2 inches (5 cm) long and matures in the fall. The scales and seed are shed, leaving only the central stem during the winter.

These trees are occasionally planted in Ohio for ornamental purposes and as Christmas trees and windbreaks. It is restricted in planting to the northern section of Ohio due to its heat intolerance. Balsam fir is quite sensitive to soil requirements. Fraser fir and Canaan fir are thought to be ecotypes of balsam fir and are preferred for Christmas tree use due to their greater heat-tolerance. Canaan fir is also more tolerant of high moisture. The ability to hold needles after being cut makes these firs desirable Christmas trees.

White (Concolor) Fir—*Abies concolor*

This is a beautiful evergreen tree from the Pacific and Rocky Mountain regions. These firs have excurrent branching patterns and have a pyramidal habit with spreading, whorled branches. Bark is usually smooth and thin on young trees, becoming thicker and more furrowed on older trees. Leaves are narrow and linear.

Needles are flat, 1–2½ inches (2½–6 cm) in length, extending outward, and curving upward on the branches. Foliage is a pleasing silver color, ranging from white to bluish-green. Leaves are stomatiferous above and below. Foliage is constricted above the base and is shed leaving a relatively smooth twig that is quite different than the spruce twig.

Flowers are monoecious, occurring in May. The fruit is a 2-inch-long (5 cm) cone that is borne upright on the branches. Cone scales are shed individually with the seed, leaving a stick protruding above the branch.

White (Concolor) Fir

29

An excellent tree for ornamental plantings, these firs develop into stately and graceful lawn specimens. It is hardy in all sections of the state and quite free from insects and diseases. Trees are very site-demanding and intolerant of excess moisture. Rocky Mountain seed sources are better adapted to Ohio conditions.

Nordmann Fir—*Abies nordmanniana*

Introduced from Asia Minor and the Balkan regions, the Nordmann fir is one of the best specimen trees for lawn and park plantings. It is a large tree, growing up to 100 feet, with distinct, spreading, pyramidal growth. Branches are spreading and whorled. Bark is smooth and thin on young trees, becoming thicker and more furrowed on older trees. Nordmann fir is sparsely planted in Ohio for specimen and ornamental purposes. Trees are site-demanding and very intolerant of poor drainage.

Needles are about 1 inch (2½ cm) in length, dark green above with a lighter cast beneath. Leaves are not conspicuously bluish-green (*stomatiferous*). Stomatic areas are usually on the lower leaf surface. Leaves of the middle rank (leaves directly above the twig) point upward and slightly forward. Needles densely cover the stem, and are glossy, and dark green. Buds are not, or only slightly, resinous.

Nordmann Fir

30

Pseudotsuga — Douglas-Fir

Douglas-firs are evergreen trees with pyramidal habits and irregularly whorled branches. Branchlets are nearly smooth but not as smooth as the branches of firs. Buds are long, pointed, and not resinous. Leaves are spirally arranged and narrow-linear in outline. Flowers are monoecious. Fruit is a pendulous cone with three-lobed bracts extending beyond the cone scales.

Key to *Pseudotsuga* Species

I. Winter buds on normal shoots are conspicuously long-pointed and brown. Buds have many scales and are non-resinous. Distinctive cones are pendulous with bracts projecting conspicuously between the cone scales. Leaves are dark or bluish-green. Douglas-firs are trees with graceful, spreading branches that are often pendulous.

Pseudotsuga menziesi (taxifolia, douglasi)— Common Douglas-Fir

Description of Species

Common Douglas-Fir—*Pseudotsuga menziesi*

The Douglas-fir is a beautiful tree that is not a true fir. It was introduced to Ohio from the Rocky Mountains and Pacific northwest regions of the United States. Trees attain a height of 200–300 feet and 3–4 feet in diameter in their native region. West of the Cascade Mountains in Washington and Oregon, the Douglas-fir is so dominant that it is almost a naturally occurring monoculture. Douglas-firs are evergreen trees with pyramidal habits and irregularly whorled branches.

Foliage is feathery soft and not sharp. The 1–1¼ inch (2½–3 cm) long, flat needles vary from blue to dark green in color. Leaves are spirally arranged and narrow-linear in outline. Branchlets are nearly smooth, but not as smooth as the branches of firs. Buds are long, pointed, and not resinous. Flowers are monoecious and bloom in May. Fruit is a pendulous cone with three-lobed bracts extending beyond the cone scales. The fruit is very distinctive and is the best identification feature when present.

Color variations from silver to heavy bluish-green are grown commercially. This is one of the best evergreens for ornamental and specimen planting on large lawns. Douglas-firs are also planted for Christmas tree purposes, commanding a premium price in Ohio. The Rocky Mountain type seems to thrive better in Ohio than the Pacific Coast form. This tree is site-demanding and disease sensitive under the wrong soil conditions. In addition, Douglas-firs are intolerant of poor drainage.

Common Douglas-Fir

Tsuga — Hemlock

Hemlocks are evergreen trees with cinnamon-red, furrowed bark and horizontal, pendulous branches. Buds are small, globose, and not resinous. Leaves are spirally arranged, usually in two ranks. Needles are about ½ inch (13 mm) long with a linear outline. Flowers are monoecious and the fruit is a small cone (less than an inch) with few scales and is showy in the fall.

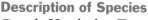

Key To *Tsuga* Species

I. Its dark green leaves are flat and arranged in two planes with white, stomatic bands on the underside of the needles. Twigs are only slightly roughened by persistent leaf bases. Branches are long, slender, and often pendulous. The tree forms a broad, pyramidal head.

Tsuga canadensis—Canada Hemlock

Description of Species

Canada Hemlock—*Tsuga canadensis*

The hemlock is a large timber tree attaining heights of more than 100 feet with trunk diameters of 2–4 feet. The tree occurs along streams and cool slopes in eastern Ohio, along the lake in Lorain County, and southward to Adams County along the Ohio River. It is also found growing native in Green and Auglaize counties. In the Hocking Hills area, the hemlocks reach the zenith of grandeur and beauty. In this scenic area, growing out of the cool ravines and deep valleys, several specimens tower above the sandstone walls 135 feet in height and 4½ feet in diameter.

The leaves are ⅓–⅔ inches (8–17 mm) in length, oblong, dark green, and lustrous on the upper surface and whitish beneath. Although the needles are spirally arranged, they appear to be two-ranked on the stem. Needles normally fall during the third year. The cones are oblong, about ¾ inch (2 cm) long, and light brown in color.

Flowers are monoecious and bloom in May. Fruit is a small cone less than an inch long with only a few scales. The cone scales are broadly ovate and are as wide as they are long. The seed is small and winged, maturing in the fall and dropping during the winter.

The hemlocks' horizontal or ascending branches and drooping twigs form a pyramidal crown. This makes it one of our most handsome and desirable evergreen trees for shade and ornament in Ohio. Unfortunately, the tree is site-demanding and difficult to grow where it is not native. Two exotic insects, including a scale insect and an adelgid, have been introduced and are destroying native stands in the northeastern United States.

The wood is light, soft, not strong, brittle, and splintery. It is used for coarse lumber and paper pulp. The bark on old trunks is cinnamon-red or dark gray, and divided into narrow, rounded ridges.

Canada Hemlock

Picea — Spruce

Spruces are evergreen trees with pyramidal habits, whorled branches, and scaly bark. Buds are small and ovoid or conical in outline. Buds may or may not be resinous. Leaves are spirally arranged. Needles are usually four-sided with stomatic lines on all sides. Flowers are monoecious. Fruit is a pendant cone with numerous, persistent scales.

Key to *Picea* Species

I. Leaves on 1-year-old twigs are rigid, sharp and pointed. They spread from the twig in all directions. Needles are borne at nearly right angles to the stem. Foliage is blue to green in color and varies by seedling or variety. Brownish-yellow bud scales curve outward and are often rolled at the apex. The cone is about 2–3 inches (5–7½ cm) long.

Picea pungens—Colorado Spruce

II. Leaves diverge from the stem at nearly right angles but in a flatter arrangement. Viewed from the end of the stem, the foliage is more semicircular.

    A. Scales on terminal winter buds are rounded and emarginate (shallow notch) or indented at the tips, especially those near the bud tip. Leaves are usually glaucous and terminate in rather abrupt, but not sharp, points. Needles have a disagreeable odor when crushed. Fruit is less than 1½ inches (4 cm) long.

Picea glauca (canadensis, alba)—White Spruce

    AA. Scales on terminal winter buds are more pointed and not emarginate at the tip. Leaves are more tapered than white spruce but not sharply pointed. Foliage is dark green and not glaucous. Branch tips are pendulous, as are cones which are 4–6 inches (10–15 cm) long.

Picea abies (excelsa)—Norway Spruce

Norway Spruce—see page 34.

33

Description of Species
Norway Spruce—*Picea abies (excelsa)*

Norway spruce is one of the most commonly planted European evergreens and was a favorite among early pioneers for plantings around homesteads. It is extensively planted in Ohio as a windbreak and for Christmas trees, though cut Norway spruce trees do not retain their foliage as well as blue or white spruce. A valuable tree for reforestation purposes on heavy, moist, clay soils of northern Ohio, the Norway spruce may escape further north and destroy native populations of native white spruce. It is the largest and longest-lived spruce for Ohio gardens. ✓

Leaves diverge from the stem at nearly right angles but in a flatter arrangement than blue spruce. Viewed from the end of the stem, the foliage is more semicircular. Leaves are more tapered than white spruce but not sharply pointed. Foliage is ½ inch (13 mm) long, dark green, and not glaucous. Scales on the terminal winter buds are more pointed and not emarginate at the tip. Flowers are monoecious and open in May. Cones are pendulous and 4–6 inches (10–15 cm) long. The cone of the Norway spruce is the largest of all the spruces and is an excellent identification feature when present.

This exotic is a large, graceful tree with reddish-brown bark and heavy, spreading branches. The branches are pendulous, or drooping, and often touch the ground. Norway spruce retains lower foliage longer than do either the blue or white spruce. The dark green foliage is quite handsome and resistant to spruce mite.

White Spruce—
Picea glauca (canadensis, alba)

White spruce is a native tree of the lake states and the New England region and extends north to the Canadian tundra. It is a large tree, ranging from 60–90 feet in height, but very narrow, or upright, when mature.

The needles are blue to light green and sometimes nearly white. Foliage is not as sharp as blue spruce and has a striking, pungent odor when crushed. Leaves diverge from the stem at nearly right angles but in a flat-

White Spruce

ter arrangement. Viewed from the end of the stem, the foliage is more semicircular than circular. Scales on terminal winter buds are rounded and emarginate at the tips. Flowers are monoecious and bloom in May. Fruit is less than 1½ inches (4 cm) long and matures in the fall.

White spruce are planted in Ohio for screens and windbreaks. In addition, the white spruce is both grown and shipped into Ohio as Christmas trees. Foliage does not hold as well when cut as do the firs and the blue spruce. White spruce is sensitive to spruce mite and high temperatures in Ohio and has a shorter life span than the blue or Norway spruces.

Colorado Spruce (Blue Spruce)—*Picea pungens*

This native of the Rocky Mountains is one of the best-known evergreens and is commonly planted for landscape purposes in Ohio. Colorado spruce has a splendid conical form for use as a lawn specimen. Height rarely exceeds 30–50 feet and the distinctive, bluish-silvery-foliaged types are the most valuable for ornamental purposes.

Foliage is green, silver, or steel blue and sharp enough to draw blood. Foliage color varies with the seedling or variety. Leaves on 1-year-old twigs are rigid and spread from the twig in all directions. Needles are borne at nearly right angles to the stem. When viewed from the end, the foliage is in a circular pattern. Brownish-yellow bud scales curve outward and are often rolled at the apex. Flowers are monoecious and bloom in May. The pendulous cone is about 2–3 inches (5–7½ cm) long and matures in the fall.

The Koster's blue spruce is one of a number of varieties selected for its foliage color and is propagated by grafting upon seedlings of Colorado spruce or other spruce species. Using the proper seed sources will increase the number of blue seedlings in the population. Colorado spruce is also grown as a premium Christmas tree and holds its needles well after being cut. Blue spruce is well-adapted to the heavy, clay soils of Ohio, and loss in the landscape is often due to windthrow.

Colorado (Blue) Spruce

35

Larix — Larch

Larch is another deciduous, coniferous tree with scaly bark. Buds are small and scaly. Leaves are entire, narrow, and flat. Foliage looks evergreen-like, is alternate, and is spirally arranged on juvenile branches. Foliage is clustered on short, lateral spurs on older twigs. Flowers are monoecious. Fruit is a small, persistent cone that is less than an inch long.

Key to *Larix* Species

I. Twigs are glabrous, reddish-yellow, and usually bloomy. Leaves are light bluish-green. Bark of the trunk and main branches is reddish-brown. Cones are less than $^{1}/_{2}$ inch (13 mm) long.

Larix laricina (americana)—Eastern Larch (Tamarack)

II Twigs are glabrous, yellow, and usually not bloomy. Leaves are soft, bright green, and ridged below. Bark of trunk is dark grayish-brown. Cones are almost 1 inch ($2^{1}/_{2}$ cm) long.

Larix decidua (europaea)—European Larch

Description of Species
European Larch—*Larix decidua*

This deciduous, evergreen conifer from Europe is better adapted to Ohio's landscape than the native larch. Cultivars such as the weeping European larch are more commonly grown for ornamental purposes. The European larch develops well on moist, heavy, loam soils. The tree grows to a height of 50–75 feet with a straight, clean trunk in a planted forest and with a broad, pyramidal crown on single specimens.

Foliage looks evergreen-like and is alternately and spirally arranged on juvenile branches. Foliage is clustered in short, lateral spurs on older twigs. Needles are flat, soft, and bluish-green in color. Leaves are 1 inch ($2^{1}/_{2}$ cm) long, entire, narrow, and flat. European larch is a conspicuous and beautiful tree in spring with new, bright green foliage.

Buds are small and scaly. Twigs are glabrous, usually not bloomy, and yellower than the native larch. Bark of the older trunk is dark grayish-brown. Flowers are monoecious and bloom in May. Fruit is a small, persistent cone less than 1 inch ($2^{1}/_{2}$ cm) long.

Eastern Larch—*Larix laricina*

The Eastern larch, also called tamarack, is a northern tree. It stands out prominently among its associates because it sheds all of its leaves in autumn. Its habit is conical and similar to spruce. The Eastern larch is found from Newfoundland, Canada, and British Columbia, Canada, to Alaska. Along with white spruce and aspen, this tree grows north into the tundra. Ohio is south of its range, but it occurs locally in the northern part of Ohio in swamps and other wet places. It is most common along borders of glacial lakes and swamps in Summit, Portage, and Stark counties. It rarely exceeds 50 feet in height and 2 feet in diameter. Wet places are its favorite home. It is too site-demanding to be useful in Ohio landscapes.

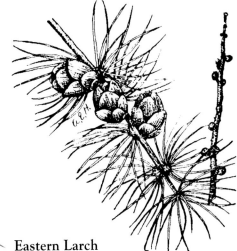

Eastern Larch

The leaves are flat, soft, slender and about 1 inch (2½ cm) long. Foliage is light bluish-green. On the twigs of the previous season's growth, needles occur singly, are alternate, and are spirally arranged on juvenile branches. On the spurs of older twigs, the foliage occurs in clusters of 10 or more. Foliage looks evergreen-like and is 1 inch (2½ cm) long. During the fall, foliage color is a distinctive golden-brown or yellow.

Flowers are monoecious. The cones are smaller than those of the European larch. Cones average ⅖ inch (1 cm) in length, bear about 12 scales, and often persist for many years.

The glossy, brown twigs are without foliage in winter and are covered with numerous stubby spurs. Twigs are glabrous, reddish-yellow, and usually bloomy. The bark on older trunks is reddish-brown and breaks up into small, round scales.

The wood is heavy, hard, and durable in contact with the soil. It is used for posts, poles, ties, and in ship building.

Pinus — Pine

Pines are evergreen trees with spreading branches that are often arranged in whorls. The bark is either furrowed or scaly. Buds are conspicuous with numerous imbricated scales. The primary leaves of seedlings are spirally arranged. The secondary leaves of landscape-sized plants are borne in bundles containing two to five needles. The number of needles per bundle, or sheath, is a useful identification feature. Flowers are monoecious. Fruit is a cone with many woody scales.

Key to *Pinus* Species

I. Needles are borne five in a bundle and are slender, minutely toothed, and soft to the touch. Needles are 2½–5½ inches (6–14 cm) long. Twigs are usually glabrous but may be hairy on young growth. Bark is purple in color on young twigs. Branches are horizontal and spreading. Older trees lose the excurrent terminal growth and assume a more open, picturesque habit. Cones are curved and more than twice as long as they are wide.

Pinus strobus—Eastern White Pine

II. Leaves (needles) are borne with less than five in a bundle.
  A. Leaves (needles) are usually three in a bundle, occasionally two.
    I. Leaves are usually in bundles of three but may have bundles of two and three on the same plant. Needles are 5–10½ inches (13–27 cm) long. Twigs are fragrant when broken. Mature bark has a vanilla-like fragrance. Cones are about 4 inches (10 cm) long and nearly as wide.

Pinus ponderosa—Ponderosa (Western Yellow) Pine

    II. Leaves are always borne with three in a bundle and are 2¾–5½ inches (7–14 cm) long. Needles are also borne in tufts on the main stem of the tree. Twigs are not fragrant when broken. Branches are horizontally arranged and form an irregular head. Cones are 3–4 inches (7½–10 cm) long and just as wide. Cones often persist for a number of years.

Pinus rigida—Pitch Pine

  AA. Leaves (needles) are always in bundles of two.
    I. Twigs are distinctly glaucous or bloomy.
      a. Leaves are dark green and 1½–2¾ inches (3½–7 cm) long. Buds are resinous. Bark of young twigs is reddish-brown, becoming shallowly fissured into scaly plates on older branches and trunks. A bushy tree with slender, horizontal branches, the pitch pine has somewhat pendulous older branches. This tree has a picturesque habit. Cones are less than 2 inches (5 cm) long and remain on the tree for years.

Pinus virginiana—Virginia (Scrub) Pine

38

aa. The dark bluish-green leaves are slender and 2¾–4¾ inches (7–12 cm) long. Bark of twigs is dark reddish-brown. Mature bark on branches and trunk breaks into large, scaly plates. Buds are not, or only slightly, resinous. Cones are 2–3 inches (5–7½ cm) long and nearly as wide as they are long.

Pinus echinata—Shortleaf Pine

11. Twigs are not glaucous or bloomy.
  a. Leaves are 5–7 inches (13–18 cm) long.
    i. Leaves are dull, dark green, and 5–7 inches (13–17 cm) long. Needles are stiff and rigid but do not break when bent. Resin ducts are internal. The trunk and larger branches are gray and broken into large plates. Cones are 3–4 inches (7½–10 cm) long and nearly as wide.

Pinus nigra—Austrian Pine

    ii. Leaves are 4–6 inches (10–15 cm) long and more slender and flexible than the Austrian pine but break when bent. Foliage is darker green than the Austrian pine and is often glossy. Resin ducts are marginal. The bark of trunks and larger branches is red-brown, giving the tree its name. Cones are 2–3 inches (5–7½ cm) long and nearly as wide as they are long.

Pinus resinosa—Red Pine

  aa. Leaves are short, 1–3 inches (2½–7½ cm) long.
    i. Leaves are bluish-green, flat, and twisted. Needles are 1¼–2¾ inches (3–7 cm) long. The tree grows to 75 feet or more, becoming irregular with age. Upper trunk and branches are salmon- or orange-colored. Cones are 1½–2 inches (4–5 cm) long and just as wide. Cones are persistent.

Pinus sylvestris—Scotch Pine

    ii. Leaves are dark to bright green, and ¾–1½ inches (2–4 cm) long. This tree may grow to 85 feet, but it is usually not more than 25–30 feet high. Young trees are sometimes shrubby. Cones are 1½–2 inches (4–5 cm) long and just as wide. Cones remain on the tree for 12–15 years.

Pinus banksiana (divaricata)—Jack Pine

Description of Species
Jack Pine—*Pinus banksiana (divaricata)*

This tree is native to the northern lake states and grows on the sterile, dry sands and poor soils of that area. Jack pine is usually planted in Ohio as a windbreak or for reforestation, rather than ornamental, purposes. The growth habit of jack pine closely resembles the Virginia pine to which it is related. Jack pine serves a similar ecological function as a pioneer invader species in the north as the Virginia pine does in southeastern Ohio.

Needles are borne two to a cluster. The foliage is ¾–1½ inches (2–4 cm) long and often twisted and stiff. Foliage is an attractive, dark green color. Cones are 1½–2 inches (4–5 cm) long and just as wide. Cones remain on the tree for 12–15 years. Cones open and spread millions of winged seeds following a fire which often kills the parent trees. Without fire, this tree is replaced by more shade-tolerant oaks and other hardwoods.

This tree may grow to heights of 85 feet but is usually no more than 30–50 feet tall. Young trees are sometimes shrubby. The trees grow rapidly while young and retain foliage to the ground for many years. Retained lower branches often result in poor form and a straggly appearance. Older trees grow much more slowly than do younger trees.

40

Jack Pine

Shortleaf Pine—*Pinus echinata*

The shortleaf pine, also known as yellow pine, hard pine, or old-field pine, is one of the more well-known commercial yellow pines of the South. Ohio is the northern limit of this plant's distribution. Slash and loblolly pines dominate the southern yellow pines in the South, but are less cold-hardy in Ohio. Similar to the other native hard pines (pitch and scrub), shortleaf pine is confined to southeastern Ohio. It occurs in Scioto, Adams, Lawrence, Jackson, Gallia, Vinton, Athens, Washington, Fairfield, Hocking, and Ross counties. Commercial stands are confined to Scioto, Jackson, Gallia, and Washington counties. In these counties, it is highly recommended as a tree for reforestation purposes.

Leaves are borne with two and sometimes three needles in a bundle. Needles are dark bluish-green and are 2¾–4¾ inches (7–12 cm) long. Foliage persists for to 2–5 years. The twigs are pale to purplish-brown and circular in cross section. Mature bark is brownish-red and broken into rectangular plates. It is thinner and lighter in color than the loblolly pine. Buds are not, or only slightly, resinous.

In the open, the young tree has a straight and somewhat stout stem with slightly ascending branches. Upon reaching maturity, the tree has a tall, straight stem and an oval crown that reaches heights of about 100 feet with a trunk diameter of about 3 feet. The young tree, when cut or burned back, reproduces itself by sprouting from the stump.

Shortleaf Pine

Male and female strobile (flowers) open in May and are both borne on the same plant. The cones are the smallest of all the Ohio yellow pines and are only 1½–2½ inches (4–6 cm) long. Cones are nearly as wide as they are long. Cones are oblong with small, sharp prickles and are generally clustered. Fruit is persistent, often holding to the twigs for 3–4 years. The small seeds are mottled and have a wing which is broadest near the center.

The wood of old trees is rather heavy, fine-grained, and hard. The lumber is often sold as hard or yellow pine. The color is yellowish-brown or orange and less resinous than that of the other important southern pines. It is used largely for interior and exterior finishing, general construction, veneers, paper pulp, excelsior, cooperage, and mine props in addition to other purposes.

41

Austrian Pine—*Pinus nigra*

Austrian pine is a native tree of Europe but is commonly planted and found growing in all sections of Ohio as a windbreak and ornamental tree. Austrian pine is well adapted to the limestone soils and heavy clays of Ohio. This is an excellent tree for windbreak planting and as specimens in large lawns, parks, and rural estates. The tree is rugged with heavy, persistent branches forming a dense crown and top growth.

Needles are borne two to a needle sheath and are flexible but do not break when bent. Foliage is 5–7 inches (13–18 cm) long and dark green. Needles are stout, rigid, slightly curved, and sharp-pointed. Foliage persists for two or more years, giving the tree a dense crown. Resin ducts are internal. One variety, the 'Corsican' (*Pinus nigra calabrica*), is a taller tree with a narrow, compact crown that has been used in forest plantings. Needles are distinctly curved and often borne in curly clusters on branches of young trees.

Twigs are not glaucous or bloomy. Mature bark is divided into large plates with dark fissures. Bark plates are light grayish-brown to almost white. Flowers are monoecious and not true flowers but open in May or early June. Cones are 4 inches (10 cm) long and oval in outline. The cones mature and are shed following the second growing season.

Pine tip blight has become a serious problem in windbreaks, forests, and shaded plantings. The first symptom is blighted branch tips, but the disease may proceed to dead branches and cause death of the host plant. Good air exchange reduces the severity of this disease. Considerable seedling variation in disease sensitivity is also seen in Austrian pine. Pesticides are labeled but marginally effective.

42

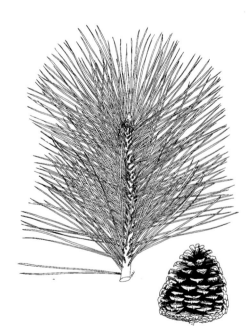

Austrian Pine

Ponderosa (Western Yellow) Pine—
Pinus ponderosa

Ponderosa pine is a large forest tree, reaching 100–200 feet in height in its native regions. This tree was introduced into Ohio from the western Rocky Mountain and Pacific Coast regions for both ornamental and reforestation purposes. The trunk of the tree grows straight and tall with stout, spreading branches forming a close, crowned top. When growing in open areas, the ponderosa pine develops a beautiful, massive top. Ponderosa pine is an attractive ornamental tree in spacious lawns or deep backgrounds where screen and windbreaks can be used.

Bark is reddish-brown, rough, scaly, and fissured on old trees. A slight odor of vanilla is detected in the bark fissures. Branches are orange to yellow in color and fragrant when broken. Flowers are monoecious and bloom in May. Cones are about 4 inches (10 cm) long and nearly as wide. The end of the cone scales terminate in a stout prickle.

Needles are usually borne in threes, but occasionally needles are borne two in a sheath. Needles are 5–10½ inches (13–27 cm) long, stiff, and dark green in color.

The Pacific Coast seed source in Secrest Arboretum, on the campus of the Ohio State University's Ohio Agricultural Research and Development Center, has suffered from drought and winter injury. The Rocky Mountain and Black Hills seed source variety, *scopulorum*, has shorter needles and dark, upright branches. The Rocky Mountain seed source produces a smaller tree but withstands the cold and soil conditions in Ohio much better. When the European settlers pushed West, they found huge areas dominated by large, widely spaced ponderosa pines growing in grasses. These areas were logged earlier in this century. Natural regeneration was allowed to replace the trees and resulted in a change in species. The original fire-dependent ecosystem of ponderosa pine is now greatly reduced and the ponderosa pine is much less common today than it was when the European settlers arrived.

Ponderosa (Western Yellow) Pine

43

Red Pine—*Pinus resinosa*

The red pine is a large forest tree of the northern pine areas and is associated with the white pine. The native range of the red pine extends south into Michigan. While this tree is not native to Ohio, it has been extensively planted for reforestation and timber growing purposes during the past 50 years. Red pine is well adapted to the thin, sterile soils and old field-types of eastern and southeastern Ohio. Pine tip blight is as severe for red pine as it is for Austrian pine.

Red pine is difficult to tell from Austrian pine in the field. The needles of the red pine break when bent, while Austrian pine needles fold over when bent. Leaves (needles) are always borne two in a bundle. Leaves are 5–7 inches (13 to 18 cm) long. Foliage is darker green than the Austrian pine and is often glossy. Resin ducts are marginal. Foliage density of Austrian pine is greater than that of red pine.

Twigs are not glaucous or bloomy. Bark of trunks and larger branches is reddish-brown, giving the tree its name. Mature bark is quite different than Austrian pine but is not seen until the tree is 30 or more years old. Fissured plates are reddish-brown in color. The Austrian pine has a more regular outline.

Flowers are monoecious and open in May. Cones of Austrian and red pines are similar in shape. At 2–3 inches (5–7½ cm) in length, the cones of the red pine are smaller than that of the Austrian pine.

This tree quickly invades cutover sites, especially in sterile, sandy soils. Mature trees may reach 75–125 feet in height. Trunks are straight and carry a broad, pyramidal crown or top. The red pine is less attractive as an ornamental tree than is the Austrian pine.

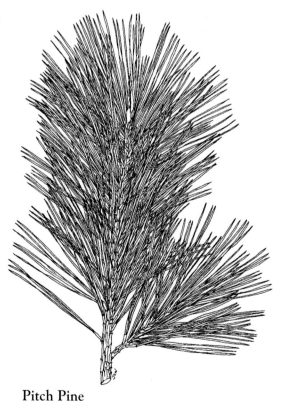

Pitch Pine

Pitch Pine—*Pinus rigida*

The pitch pine grows on dry ridges and slopes of the hilly regions of southeastern Ohio. It occurs scattered or in small groups with hardwoods or other pines in practically every county from Fairfield south to the Ohio River. It is also reported to occur sparingly in Columbiana, Jefferson, Belmont, Guernsey, and Licking counties.

As a native pine, it has excellent possibilities for reforestation purposes on the worn-out sandstone and shale soils of southeastern Ohio. It commonly attains heights of 50–75 feet and a diameter of 1–2 feet. The trunk is erect and at heights of 20–30 feet branches into a close head made up of large branches and noticeably thick foliage. Pitch pine has longer leaves, larger cones, and generally a rougher and less straight trunk than the shortleaf pine with which is it often found. Branches are horizontally arranged and form an irregular head.

The leaves, which are found in clusters of three, are 2¾–5½ inches (7–14 cm) long. Needles are stiff, dark yellowish-green in color, and stand out straight from the twigs. They fall during the second year. Small branch stubs are borne on the main stems with clusters of foliage.

Twigs are not fragrant when broken. The cones are 3–4 inches (7½–10 cm) long and light brown in color. Cones are persistent and usually cling to the branches for several years, sometimes for as many as 10–12 years. Intermediate bark on the stems and branches is rough. Mature bark is gray or reddish-brown and irregularly divided into broad, flat, continuous ridges.

The wood is light, soft, and brittle. It is sawed into lumber for general construction. This tree is able to grow in very poor soil and has the capacity, when young, of sprouting successfully from the base of the stump when burned or cut back. This is an uncommon trait among conifers.

Eastern White Pine—*Pinus strobus*

The white pine occurs naturally in the lake-states region eastward to the Northern Atlantic states, and southward throughout the Appalachian Mountain section of Eastern North America. In Ohio, it is confined to a portion of the northeastern section of the state.

When found, it is present only in small areas, occurring most abundantly near the headwaters of the Mohican River in southern Ashland County. It has been found in Ashtabula, Lake, Cuyahoga, Geauga, Trumbull, Summit, Lorain, Erie, Ashland, Holmes, Coshocton, Knox, Belmont, and Jefferson counties. It grows on high, dry, sandy, and rocky ridges but prefers cooler, moister situations.

The trunk is straight with branches that extend horizontally in whorls (a number of branches are attached at a single level around the stem). The whorls mark the successive years of upward growth. Older trees lose the excurrent terminal growth and assume a more open and picturesque habit. The tree commonly attains heights of 75–100 feet and diameters of 2–3 feet, though much larger specimens can be found.

The leaves are 2½–5½ inches (6–14 cm) long, bluish-green on the upper surface, and white beneath. Needles occur in bundles of five, which distinguishes it from all other eastern pines. Leaves are slender, minutely toothed, and soft to the touch.

Twigs are usually glabrous but may be hairy on young growth. Bark is purple on young twigs. The intermediate bark is thin and greenish-gray on young trees, while the mature bark is thick, deeply furrowed, and grayish-brown.

Flowers are monoecious and open in May. Cones are curved and more than twice as long as they are wide. The cone is 4–6 inches (10–15 cm) long and cylindrical with thin, usually very gummy, scales containing small, winged seeds which require two years to mature. The cones are not armed with prickles.

Its rapid growth, tolerance of Ohio growing conditions, and the high quality of the wood make it one of the most desirable trees for forest planting. The

Eastern White Pine

Eastern White Pine

wood is light and soft but not strong. The color is light brown, often tinged with red, and easily worked. It is in demand for construction purposes, box boards, and other products.

The white pine's straight stem, regular pyramidal shape, and soft, grayish-green foliage make it universally appreciated as an ornamental tree. The soft needles and flexible branch tips make it less popular as a Christmas tree than the Scotch pine. Its tolerance of growing conditions in Ohio makes it the most widely planted pine for landscape applications. White pine is more tolerant of serious insect and diseases than other pines in Ohio, but it is very sensitive to road-salt damage and should be planted away from heavily salted roadways.

Scotch Pine—*Pinus sylvestris*

Scotch pine, or Scot's pine, is a native tree of Europe but is extensively planted in Ohio for ornamental, windbreak, and Christmas tree purposes. Several seed sources have been introduced from Europe. Selections have been made based on color retention during the winter months in order to increase this plant's marketability as a Christmas tree. This is the most popular Christmas tree in Ohio but does not retain the pyramidal growth pattern without an annual pruning. Scotch pine has escaped cultivation in several areas of Ohio and easily becomes naturalized. This tree was commonly planted around homesteads by early settlers and is often found as large trees near buildings with Austrian pine and Norway spruce as associates. Trees grow to 75 feet or more, becoming irregularly shaped with age.

Leaves are always in bundles of two. Foliage is bluish-green, flat, and twisted. Needles are 1¼–2¾ inches (3–7 cm) long. Flowers are monoecious and bloom in May. Cones are 1½–2 inches (4–5 cm) long and just as wide. Cones are persistent.

Bark is reddish-brown, thin, and scaly in younger trees. Intermediate bark is exfoliating (scaly) and ranges in color from a reddish-brown to a showy copper. Mature bark is deeply furrowed and a dark grayish-brown color. Trunks are usually irregular and crooked.

Scotch pines grow vigorously as a reforestation tree on poor soil sites when young, but growth decreases rapidly in later years. The shrubby habit of the Christmas tree seed sources make this tree undesirable as a timber tree in Ohio, although this is a major timber species in Europe. Pine tip blight is a slightly less severe problem for Scotch pine than for Austrian and red pines, but it can still be fatal. Other foliar diseases cause more serious problems for Scotch than for the Austrian and white pines which are found more commonly in Ohio landscapes.

Scotch Pine

Virginia (Scrub) Pine—*Pinus virginiana*

The Virginia, scrub, or Jersey pine is the most common and widely distributed of any of the native pines in southeastern Ohio. It is confined to the sandstone soils of the state extending from Columbiana County southward to Lawrence, Scioto, and Adams counties. In sections of Washington, Athens, Jackson, Lawrence, and Scioto counties it occupies extensive areas of old fields and washed, gullied lands. Usually it is found growing in pure stands and is very persistent in establishing itself on worn-out, abandoned, and sterile soils.

Scrub pine is a bushy tree with slender, horizontal, and somewhat pendulous branches. It is one of the slower growing pines. The side branches usually persist for many years even after dying, thus giving a scrubby appearance to the tree which is responsible for one of its common names. This tree has a picturesque habit.

The twisted and spreading leaves are borne two in a cluster. Needles vary from 1½–2¾ inches (4–7 cm) long and are deep green in color. Virginia pine needles are shorter than those of any other pine native to the state.

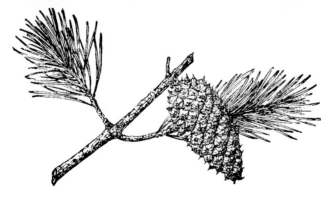

Virginia (Scrub) Pine

Populus — Poplar

Poplars are deciduous trees with rounded or angled branches. Leaves may be alternate, lobed, toothed, or entire. Buds are imbricate with many scales. Flowers are dioecious and borne in pendulous catkins. Fruit is a capsule containing seeds with basal hairs that allow the seeds to be carried by the wind.

Key to *Populus* Species

I. Leaf stalks are not flattened vertically and are rounded, or nearly so.

    A. Leaves are lobed, white, and woolly below. Foliage is toothed or shallow-lobed, especially on vigorous shoots. Young twigs and buds are often white and woolly.

        Populus alba—White Poplar

    AA. Leaves are not lobed.

        I. Leaves are whitish and hairy beneath. Foliage is 4¾–6½ inches (12–16½ cm) long, dark green, and slightly hairy above. Terminal bud is sticky and usually much larger than side buds. Twigs are fragrant. First scale of side bud is borne on the side opposite the twig.

            Populus ✕gileadensis—Balm of Gilead Poplar

        II. Oval leaves are light green beneath and 4–7¼ inches (10–18½ cm) long. Foliage is tomentose when young, becoming glabrous, or somewhat hairy, as it ages. Branchlets are stout and dull brown or gray in color. Bud is slightly sticky.

            Populus heterophylla—Swamp Poplar   *Cottonwood*

II. Leaf stalk is flattened vertically.

    A. Leaves have translucent borders.

        I. Tree has a narrow and upright habit. The individual branches are ascending. Leaves are usually narrow and wedge-shaped at the base.

            Populus nigra 'Italica'—Lombardy Poplar

        II. Tree has a widespreading habit, not narrow and upright.

            a. Side buds curve away from the twig. The third bud scale is nine-tenths as long as the bud. Buds are small and viscid. Twigs are glabrous and slightly angled. Leaves are usually broad and rounded to wedge shaped at the base. No gland is present at base of the leaf blade.

               Populus ✕canadensis—Carolina Poplar

            aa. Side buds do not curve away from the twig. The third bud scale is not over three-fourths as long as the bud. Leaves are usually square or nearly heart-shaped at the base.

               i. Twigs are slightly angled. Leaves are 2¾–4¾ (7–12 cm) long with glands present at base of leaf blade.

Populus deltoides (monilifera, balsamifera)—Eastern Poplar (Northern Cottonwood)

ii. Twigs are strongly angled. Leaves are larger, 4–6½ inches (10–16½ cm) long, with glands present at base of leaf blade.

Populus deltoides missouriensis—Southern Poplar

AA. Leaves are without translucent borders.
    I. Leaves are finely toothed and thin. Foliage is 1¼–2¾ inches (5¾–7 cm) long, glabrous, and often slightly bloomy beneath. Buds have a brown, varnished appearance, and are often curved toward the twig. Twigs are glabrous, shiny, and reddish-brown in color.

Populus tremuloides—Quaking Aspen

    II. Leaves are coarsely toothed and thick. When young, foliage is 2¼–4 inches (7–10 cm) long, dark green above, and gray and woolly beneath. Foliage is nearly bloomy when mature. Buds are often divergent from the twig. Twigs and buds are gray and hairy. Twigs finally become reddish or orange-brown in color when mature.

Populus grandidentata—Bigtooth Aspen

Description of Species
White (Silver) Poplar—*Populus alba*

White poplar was introduced from Europe and Asia but has become naturalized. Silver poplar is longer lived than some of the other poplars. It is a large tree, standing 75–100 feet in height with a massive, broad head. Like many other members of the genus, it is undesirable for ornamental purposes because the roots often clog older underground tile and drains. Plastic pipe is resistant to damage.

Bark is gray to light green or white with black, diamond-shaped scars on old trunks. The bark and foliage color give the tree its common name. Young twigs and buds are often white and woolly as well. Leaf petioles (stalks) are not flattened vertically and are rounded, or nearly so. Leaves are three- to five-lobed, and coarsely toothed, especially on vigorous shoots. Foliage color is dark green above with thick, white or silver hairs covering the lower surface.

Carolina Poplar

Carolina Poplar—*Populus* ×*canadensis*

The Carolina poplar has a widespreading habit and is not narrow or upright. This tree is widely scattered and does not occur in great abundance except when planted in cities and towns for shade. It is unsatisfactory for shade because it begins to shed its leaves by midsummer, and limbs are easily broken by wind. Aggressive growth of the roots often results in clogging of drainage tiles and drain pipes that do not have cemented joints.

The leaves are simple, alternate, and ovate or triangular in outline. Leaf bases are more rounded than square, while leaf margins are finely toothed. Leaves are a shiny, dark green above, paler beneath, and 2–4 inches (5–10 cm) in length and width. Leaves are supported by flattened, slender petioles that are 1½–3 inches (4–8 cm) long. No gland is present at the base of the leaf blade.

The winter buds are conical, pointed, and ½–¾ inch (1–2 cm) long. Buds are covered with chestnut brown, resinous scales. Side buds curve away from the twig. The third bud scale is nine-tenths as long as the bud. Buds are small and viscid (sticky). The twigs are smooth and yellow to yellowish-green in color. Twigs are moderately stout and slightly angled.

The pendant male flowers are borne in dense catkins and appear before the leaves. Female flowers are also in catkins but have fewer flowers per cluster. Seeds mature before the leaves. Carolina poplar is a cross between the black poplar and the cottonwood and is best described as a series of cultivars. 'Eugenei' is a male clone and thus would not produce fruit.

Eastern Poplar (Cottonwood)—*Populus deltoides*

Cottonwood is a large tree, sometimes 100 feet high and 3–4 feet in diameter, with large, upright, spreading branches forming an open, broad crown. It is one of the most rapidly growing native Ohio trees, common in floodplains and swampy areas.

This tree is distributed over the entire state and attains great size when growing along rich bottom lands and in major drainage valleys. In northwestern Ohio, the poplar, or cottonwood, is a common associate of forest trees such as elm, green ash, sycamore, silver maple, red oak, and swamp white oak.

The leaves are simple, alternate, 2¾–4¾ inches (7–12 cm) long, and 2½–5 inches (6–13 cm) wide. The leaf blade is broadly triangular in shape with a translucent margin. Leaves are pointed with coarsely toothed margins, which are somewhat rounded and curved. The mature leaf surface is smooth, except along the margins which tend to be somewhat hairy. Foliage color is shiny green above and somewhat paler and smooth below. Leaf bases are usually square, or nearly heart-shaped. Petioles are flattened and 1½–3 inches (4–7½ cm) long. Leaves have glands present at the base of the leaf blade.

The twigs are stout, angular, smooth, and yellowish-brown in color. Buds are slender with a conical-shape. Terminal buds are resinous and ½–¾ inch (1¼–2 cm) long. The terminal bud is often five-angled. Side buds do not curve away from the twig. The third bud scale is not over three-fourths as long as the bud. On young

Eastern Poplar (Cottonwood)

51

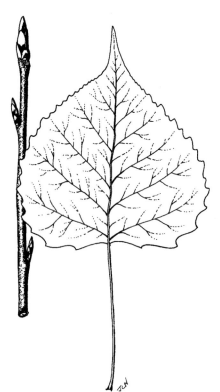

Eastern Poplar (Cottonwood)

trees, the bark is light greenish-yellow and smooth, gradually becoming ash gray and deeply furrowed on mature trees.

The flowers appear before the leaves. Pollen-bearing flowers and seed-producing flowers occur on different trees. Female flowers produce large amounts of seed with basal hairs in June. The fruit is a three- to four-valved capsule arranged in drooping tassels. The seed looks something like a dandelion seed and is borne by the wind for great distances. Seeds may occur in sufficient numbers to turn the ground beneath the tree white.

The wood is soft, not durable, and warps easily but is suitable for various uses such as boxes, crates, shelves, lath, sheathing, and wooden ware. It is highly prized by paper manufacturers who use the pulpwood for the manufacture of the highest-grade, gloss magazine and book paper.

Southern Poplar—*Populus deltoides missouriensis*

Distribution of the southern poplar is confined more to the southern portion of the state along flood plains and stream valleys. Like the cottonwood, the southern poplar can be a massive tree. They can reach 100 feet in height and have a trunk 3–4 feet in diameter. The tree is upright with large, spreading branches forming an open, broad crown.

Southern poplar is a tree that is similar to the Eastern poplar except that the twigs are smaller and the branches are more angled. Leaves are 4–6½ inches (10–16½ cm) long, larger than those of the cottonwood, with glands present at the base of the leaf blade. The leaf margins have translucent borders and toothed margins. Leaves are not typically triangular in shape, but are broadly ovate or round.

Balm of Gilead Poplar—*Populus* ×*gileadensis*

Probably introduced from Asia, the Balm of Gilead poplar attains a height between 50–75 feet and has spreading branches. This tree may be a hybrid between *P. deltoides* and *P. balsamifera*. Bark is gray and smooth. Buds are covered with a varnish-like, sticky resin and are quite pleasant to smell. Twigs are reddish-brown in color and have terminal buds that are ½ inch (13 mm) long and usually much larger than side buds. The first scale of the side bud is borne on the side opposite the twig. Twigs are fragrant.

Leaves are not lobed, but are broad and have a cordate leaf base. Leaves are 4¾–6½ inches (12–16½ cm) in length, and about 3 inches (7½ cm) wide. Foliage has a dark green color with whitish hairs beneath the leaf becoming dense along the veins. Less pubescence is present on the upper leaf surface. Petioles are not flattened but are rounded, or nearly so.

Monoecious flowers open in March or April. Since this is a sterile clone, seedlings are not a problem. Despite the fact that the tree is sterile, it has escaped cultivation in many areas of Ohio as it spreads by suckers. Like other members of the genus, it is undesirable for ornamental purposes because the roots often clog underground tile drains, although modern, plastic sewer pipes with cemented joints are not harmed. Wind damage is common as well.

Bigtooth Aspen (Poplar)—
Populus grandidentata

This tree is nearly as common as the quaking aspen and grows in association with it. This aspen is a rapid grower that sometimes reaches a height of 80 feet and a diameter of 20 inches.

It is a tree that prefers moist, sandy, rich soils, especially along the borders of streams, ponds, and lakes. Its natural range extends from Nova Scotia, Canada, westward to Minnesota, southward to the Ohio River, and along the Appalachians to North Carolina. In Ohio, it is uniformly distributed throughout the state.

The bark is smooth and greenish-gray in color. The mature bark of older trees is dark and divided into broad, flat ridges at the root crown. The buds are gray, downy, and somewhat larger than those of the other species of aspen. Twigs are gray and pubescent when young, becoming reddish- to orangish-brown at maturity.

The leaves distinguish this species from the quaking aspen. Leaf blades are up to 2¼–4 inches (5¾–10 cm) long, dark green above, and gray and woolly beneath when young. Foliage is nearly bloomy when mature. In contrast to the regular- and fine-toothed edges of the quaking aspen, the edges are coarsely and irregularly toothed. Like the quaking aspen, this tree lacks the translucent borders seen in other poplars.

The flowers are in catkins similar to those of the other poplar species. Pollen-bearing flowers and seed-producing flowers occur on different trees. The pollen-bearing flowers are arranged in drooping catkins, 1½–2½ inches (4–6 cm) long. The wood is light brown with thin, weak, soft, and nearly white sapwood. It is used in the manufacturer of paper, excelsior, and, to a small extent, woodenware.

Swamp Poplar (Cottonwood)—*Populus heterophylla*

This is a tree of low, wet swamps and the flood plains of the larger streams and rivers. It is reported from Ashtabula County westward to the old black-swamp areas of northwestern Ohio and south to the Ohio River.

The seeds are carried far by winds and germinate on wet sandy soils. The tree attains a height of 70–90 feet and a diameter of 3 feet. Branchlets are stout and dull brown or gray in color. Buds are slightly sticky. The branches are usually short, forming a narrow, round-topped crown.

Bigtooth Aspen (Poplar)

53

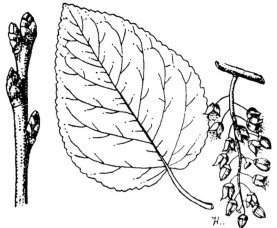

The leaves are broadly ovate, 3–6 inches (7½–15 cm) wide and 4–7¼ inches (10–18 cm) long. The leaf blade gradually narrows at the tip and is slightly rounded toward the base. Margins are usually finely toothed. Foliage is dark green above and pale and smooth below. Foliage is tomentose when young, becoming glabrous or somewhat hairy as it ages. Petioles (leaf stems) are round and 2–3 inches (5–7½ cm) long.

The flowers bloom in early spring and are in catkins. Female catkins have few flowers, while the male catkins are larger and many-flowered. The fruit contains the tiny seeds supported by "cotton" and is borne on female, or pistillate, trees. Male trees produce no fruit, and the flowers are shed after pollen is shed. The fruit ripens before leaves are full-grown. The male and female flowers occur on different trees.

The wood is light and soft. The wood requires special attention while drying in order to prevent warping. Swamp poplar makes good paper pulp. Like other members of the genus, the roots often clog older underground tile and drains. Moist areas may require a tree such as this that is adapted to low oxygen soils.

Swamp Poplar (Cottonwood)

Lombardy Poplar—*Populus nigra "Italica"*

Lombardy poplar is an upright, ascending cultivar of the European black poplar that was introduced from Europe and western Asia. Branches are closely pressed to the main trunk, growing nearly upright, and forming a narrow crown or head. This cultivar grows rapidly and has been used principally in gardens for screens and tall backgrounds.

Leaves have a flattened petiole. The leaf blade is 2–3 inches (5–7½ cm) long and triangular in shape with a translucent border. Leaves are medium green with a wedge-shaped base. This tree is very short-lived, rarely living more than 10–15 years. Lombardy poplar is attacked by a number of canker-causing fungi that cause decline and death in a few years. Fungicides are not effective.

Lombardy Poplar

husk

Eastern Black Walnut—*Juglans nigra*

This valuable forest tree occurs on rich bottom lands and moist, fertile hillsides throughout the state. In the forest, the black walnut frequently attains heights of 100 feet with a straight stem, clear of branches halfway up the tree. Growing in open areas, the stem is short and the crown is broad and spreading.

The leaves are alternate and odd-pinnately compound. Leaves are 1–2 feet (30½–61 cm) long, and have 15–23 leaflets. Foliage is a yellowish-green color. The leaflets are about 3 inches (7½ cm) long, lanceolate in outline, and irregularly toothed along the margin. Leaf scars lack a hairy, felt-like margin on the upper edge of the leaf scar.

Buds have few scales. Terminal buds are smaller than the butternut and about ⅓ inch (8 mm) long. Lateral buds are smaller than the terminal buds. Pith in the twigs is buff-colored and chambered after the first season. The bark is thick, dark brown in color, and divided by rather deep fissures into rounded ridges.

Black walnut and butternut are allelopathic and produce a compound called juglone. This compound will injure some other plants. Many plants in the rose family and heath family are very sensitive and will be injured or killed if planted beneath the drip line of a black walnut tree. Other plants such as bluegrass grow very well beneath the crowns of black walnut or butternut trees.

Flowers are monoecious. Male flowers are borne in long catkins. Female flowers are rounded and have conspicuous, red-fringed stigmas. The fruit is a large drupe with a two- to four-celled nut. The fruit is borne singly or in pairs and enclosed in a solid green husk which does not split open even after the nut is ripe. The nut itself is black with a very hard, thick, finely ridged shell, enclosing a rich, oily kernel which is edible and highly nutritious. This tree produces the black walnut nuts of commerce, but the fruit is considered a liability in an urban site. Walnut trees are easily propagated from the nuts. Seedlings grow rapidly on good soils.

The heartwood is of superior quality and value. Black walnut is the most valuable timber species in Ohio. It is heavy, hard, strong, and of a rich, chocolate brown color. Freedom from warping and checking, acceptance of a high polish, and durability make it highly prized for a great variety of uses, including furniture and cabinet work, gun stocks, and airplane propellers. Small trees are mostly sapwood, which is light-colored and not durable. Urban trees have no timber value since they may contain metal, such as nails, in the wood.

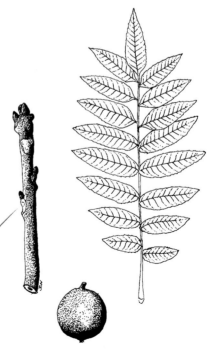

Eastern Black Walnut

63

Carya — Hickory

Hickories are deciduous trees with branches having solid pith. Terminal buds bear imbricate, scaly buds except in the bitternut hickory which has valvate or foliate buds. Leaves are alternate with the leaflets arranged in an odd-pinnate pattern. Male flowers are borne in catkins. Female flowers are borne on the same tree (monoecious) but are inconspicuous. Fruit is a husked nut and is often edible.

Key to *Carya* Species

I. Buds are valvate to foliate and sulphur yellow in color. Leaflets are 3¼–6 inches (8½–15 cm) long. Five to nine leaflets are borne in an odd-pinnate pattern. Leaf scars are large and broad.

Carya (Hicoria) cordiformis—Bitternut Hickory

II. Buds have overlapping scales. Three to nine leaflets are borne in an odd-pinnate pattern. Branches are stout and coarse. Leaf scars are large and circular.

A. Terminal buds are small, ¼–½ inch (6–13 mm) long.

I. Branchlets and leaflets are glabrous. Leaves have three to seven, usually five, leaflets. Bark is dark gray, fissured, and tightly held.

Carya (Hicoria) glabra—Pignut Hickory

II. Branchlets and leaflets are scarcely pubescent. Leaves have five to seven, usually five, leaflets. Bark is dark gray, fissured, and closely held.

Carya (Hicoria) ovalis—Red Hickory

AA. Terminal buds are larger and are ½–1 inch (13–25 mm) or longer.

I. Twigs are densely woolly, or hairy, and bright brown in color. Leaves contain seven to nine leaflets. Foliage is very fragrant when crushed. Bark is ridged and closely held.

Carya (Hicoria) tomentosa—Mockernut Hickory

II. Twigs are glabrous, or only slightly hairy, when young. Bark is shaggy and breaks into plates that are shed.

a. Leaves have five, rarely seven, leaflets. The upper leaflets are larger than the lower ones. Twigs have light reddish-brown bark.

Carya (Hicoria) ovata— Shagbark Hickory

aa. Leaves have seven to nine leaflets. Twigs have orange bark.

Carya (Hicoria) laciniosa—Shellbark Hickory

Description of Species
Bitternut Hickory—
Carya (Hicoria) cordiformis

The bitternut hickory is a tall tree with a broad, pyramidal crown, attaining a height of 100 feet and a diameter of 2–3 feet. This tree is common throughout the state and is found in moist forests and flood plains. It is well known by its round, bitter nuts. Hickories with valvate or foliate buds are known as pecan hickories and are generally vase-shaped in habit.

The bark on the trunk is granite gray, faintly tinged with yellow, and less rough than most other hickories. Bark is broken into thin, plate-like scales. The winter buds are valvate to foliate, scurfy, bright yellow, and quite different from those of other hickories. The winter bud is an outstanding identification feature. This tree is more closely related to pecan than to shagbark hickory.

The leaves are alternate and odd-pinnately compound. Leaves are from 6–10 inches (15–25 cm) long and composed of five to nine leaflets. The individual leaflets are 3¼–6 inches (8½–15 cm) long and smaller and more slender than those of the other hickories. Leaf scars are large and broad.

The flowers, like those of all the hickories, are of two kinds on the same tree. Male catkins are conspicuous, while the female flowers are small and easily overlooked. The fruit is about 1 inch (2½ cm) long and thin-husked. The nut itself usually has a thin shell that is brittle. The kernel is very bitter and not considered edible. The wood is hard, strong, and heavy.

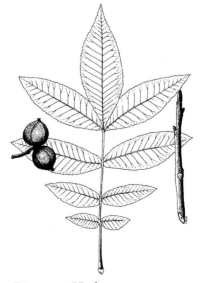

Bitternut Hickory

65

Pignut Hickory—*Carya (Hicoria) glabra*

The pignut hickory is a medium to large, upland tree occurring plentifully in all parts of the state. It has a tapering trunk and a narrow, oval head.

Mature bark is closely held, ridged, and dark gray but occasionally is rough and flaky. The twigs are thin, smooth, and glossy brown. The polished, brown winter buds are egg-shaped. Branches are stout and coarse. The outer, reddish-brown scales fall in the autumn. Overwintering buds have overlapping scales. Terminal buds are small and only ¼–½ inch (6–13 mm) long. Leaf scars are large and circular.

The leaves are smooth, 8–12 inches (20–30½ cm) long, and composed of five to seven, usually five, leaflets. Leaflets are borne in an odd-pinnate pattern. The individual leaflets are 3–6 inches (7½–15 cm) long and 1–2 inches (2½–5 cm) wide. Fall color is a golden yellow.

Flowers are monoecious. Male flowers are catkins and showy, while the female flowers are green and inconspicuous. Flowering occurs in May. The fruit is pear-shaped or rounded, usually with a neck at the base. Thin husks split only half way to the base or not at all. The nut is smooth, light brown in color, rather thick-shelled, and has an edible kernel. The wood is heavy, hard, strong, tough, and flexible. Pignut hickory lumber uses are the same as those of the other hickories.

Pignut Hickory

Shellbark Hickory—*Carya (Hicoria) laciniosa*

The shellbark hickory, or king nut hickory, is primarily confined to central and southern Ohio and is rare in the northern part of the state. It is similar in appearance to the shagbark hickory, but is smaller in stature. It is a distinct tree of coves and richer slopes. Shellbark hickories tolerate moister sites than do the shagbark hickory. The lower branches of this stately hickory are drooping and clothed with large leaves.

Twigs are much stouter and glabrous, or only slightly hairy, when young with orangish-brown bark. The bark of the trunk is shaggy with long thin strips separating from the trunk, as does the shagbark hickory. The winter terminal buds are imbricate and sometimes nearly 3 inches (7½ cm) in length.

Shellbark Hickory

The leaves are alternate, odd-pinnately compound, and vary from 10–24 inches (25–61 cm) in length. Leaves are composed of five to nine, usually seven, leaflets on a leaf stalk that is abruptly thickened at the base. The leaf base remains after the leaflets fall and often curls backward. The oblong to lanceolate leaflets are larger than shagbark hickory and range from 4–10 inches (10–25 cm) in length.

Flowers are monoecious. Male flowers are catkins and showy, while the female flowers are green and inconspicuous. Flowering occurs in May. The fruit of this species is a nut enclosed in a thick, hard husk that splits into several pieces. It is prominently four- to six-ridged, or angled, and somewhat flattened. The nuts are larger than shagbark hickory and are borne singly or in pairs. Nuts average from 1–2 inches (2½–5 cm) in length. The kernel of the shellbark hickory is light brown, sweet, and in demand as a food. Shellbark hickory is second in popularity to pecan.

The wood differs little from that of the shagbark hickory. It is heavy, hard, tough, very strong, and used for many purposes requiring a wood of unusual strength, hardness, and toughness. Hickories produce excellent firewood.

Red Hickory—*Carya (Hicoria) ovalis*

The red hickory tree is very similar to the pignut hickory. It thrives in the same areas as the pignut, and is often hard to distinguished from the pignut hickory. Many people consider red hickory to be a northern ecotype of the pignut hickory. At maturity, the red hickory attains a height of 50–80 feet with a trunk diameter of from 2–3 feet. The crown is narrowly oblong with rather short, spreading branches. Lower branches are drooping. The trunk extends straight into the crown and is often forked.

Buds are small and only ¼–½ inch (6–13 mm) long. Branchlets and leaflets are scarcely pubescent. The bark is dark gray, fissured, and closely held on young trees. Mature bark separates into narrow, shaggy plates on older trunks, but even these plates are more tightly held than shagbark and shellbark hickories. This character give rise to the name of false-shagbark hickory.

The leaves are 8–12 inches (20–30½ cm) long. They are composed of five to seven leaflets which are oblong or rounded to lance-shaped, 3–5 inches (7½–13 cm) long, and 1–2 inches (2½–5 cm) wide. Leaflets sharply taper at the apex and are finely serrate, or toothed, along the margin.

Flowers are monoecious. Male flowers are catkins and showy, while the female flowers are green and inconspicuous. Flowering occurs in May. The fruit is subglobose, from ⅘–1 inch (20–25 mm) long, and four-channeled from the apex to the base. Fruits are light brown and scaly when ripe. The husk is thin and is difficult to split. The nut is brownish in color with a small, sweet kernel.

This tree is found on lower slopes of southeastern Ohio rather than the ridges where the pignut hickory is found. Red hickory is particularly common on southern and western exposures. The wood is heavy, strong, and hard. It is reddish-brown in color which gives this plant its local name of red hickory. It is said to be somewhat inferior to the other hickories but is used for the same purposes.

Shagbark Hickory

Shagbark Hickory—*Carya (Hicoria) ovata*

The shagbark hickory is well-known because of its sweet and delicious nuts. It is a large, commercial tree, averaging 60–100 feet high and 1–2 feet in trunk diameter. The shagbark hickory thrives on rich, damp soil and is common along streams and on moist hillsides throughout the state.

The terminal winter buds are egg-shaped and ½–1 inch (13–25 mm) long. Outer bud scales have narrow tips on the scales. Twigs are glabrous, or only slightly hairy, when young and have a light reddish-brown color. The bark of the trunk is rougher on shagbark and shellbark than on the other hickories. Mature bark color is light gray, and the bark separates into thick plates which are only slightly attached to the tree. The mature bark gives this tree its common name.

The leaves are alternate, odd-pinnately compound, and from 8–15 inches (20–38 cm) long. Leaves are composed of five, and rarely seven, obovate to ovate leaflets. The upper leaflets are larger than the lower ones.

The flowers are monoecious and open after the leaves have nearly attained their full size. The globular fruit matures in November and is borne singly or in pairs. The husk is thick and deeply grooved at the seams. The nut is compressed and pale. The shell of the nut is thin, and the kernel is sweet. The kernel can be used as a substitute for pecan but is less favored than shellbark hickory.

Littlenut shagbark hickory, *Carya (Hicoria) tomentosa nutalli*, is a variety of the common shagbark, although the bark and form of the tree show practically no difference. This variety is identified entirely by the shape and size of the fruit. The nut is described as being "rounded." It is rarely pointed at top, although it may be either rounded or abruptly pointed at the base. The nut is heavily compressed, sharply angled, and about ¾ inch (2 cm) long and ½ inch (13 mm) thick.

The wood is heavy, hard, tough, and very strong. It is used largely in the manufacture of agricultural implements and tool handles. For fuel, the hickories are the most satisfactory of our native trees. The dense wood gives off much heat.

Hickories are tolerant of construction and human activity. This tree is likely to survive the construction of a home on the site. Trees in a landscape often predate the home. Hickories are slow growing and difficult to transplant, thus this tree is rarely found in nurseries.

Mockernut Hickory—
Carya (Hicoria) tomentosa (alba)

The mockernut, white hickory, whiteheart, or bigbud hickory is commonly found on well-drained soils throughout the state. It is tall, short-limbed, and averages 60 feet in height and 1–2 feet in trunk diameter. The tree has an upright habit even when grown in the open.

The winter buds are about an inch (2 cm) long, round, or broadly egg-shaped, and covered with downy, hard scales. The recent twigs are short, stout, and more or less covered with downy hairs. Twigs are bright brown in color. The mature bark is dark gray, hard, closely, and deeply furrowed, often apparently cross furrowed or netted. Bark is closely held and very different than the shellbark and shagbark hickories.

Odd-pinnately compound leaves contain seven to nine leaflets. Leaves range from 6–12 inches (15–30½ cm) long. The upper leaflets are larger than the lower ones. Foliage is very fragrant when crushed. Foliage is densely pubescent beneath, giving rise to the scientific name.

The flowers, like those of all other hickories, are monoecious. The male flowers are borne in three-branched catkins. Female flowers are borne in clusters of two to five in May. The fruit is oval, or nearly round, to slightly pear-shaped. Fruits have a very thick, strong-scented husk which splits nearly to the base when ripe. The nut is of various forms, but is sometimes four- to six-ridged. The color is light brown and the nut has a very thick shell with a small, sweet kernel.

Mockernut Hickory

Betula — Birch

Birches are deciduous trees with scaly buds. Leaves are borne in an alternate pattern and are toothed. Flowers are monoecious and borne in catkins. Fruits are small, winged nuts borne in strobiles, or cones.

Key to *Betula* Species

I. Leaves and 1-year-old twigs are aromatic when crushed.

    A. One-year twigs and buds are glossy with a uniform, brown color. The bark of the trunk is glossy, smooth, and brown or black. Buds are somewhat pointed and sharp. Twigs are a source of the oil of wintergreen.

        Betula lenta—Sweet Birch

    AA. One-year-old twigs are gray to greenish-brown and lighter in color than the buds. Mature trunks have yellow, flaky bark. Buds are rather blunt and not sharp.

        Betula alleghaniensis (lutea)—Yellow Birch

II. Leaves and 1-year-old twigs are not aromatic when crushed.

    A. Leaves are glaucous (bloomy) beneath with seven to nine pairs of veins. Intermediate bark is tan to cinnamon-brown and exfoliates in papery flakes.

        Betula nigra—River Birch

    AA. Leaves are green beneath with three to seven pairs of veins per leaf. Foliage is triangular in shape. Bark on trunks is white and exfoliating. Branches are usually somewhat pendulous.

    Betula pendula (verrucosa, alba)—European White Birch

Description of Species
Yellow Birch—*Betula alleghaniensis (lenta)*

The yellow birch is the most valuable birch of New England. In Ohio, it has been found locally in Ashtabula County, and south to Scioto and Adams counties. Yellow birch is often found in association with hemlock in Ohio. It requires the cool, moist soils of north-facing slopes.

The leaves are simple, alternate, and oval to oblong in outline. Foliage is 3–5 inches (7½–13 cm) long. Foliage is dark green and lusterless on the upper leaf surface. Leaf margins are doubly and finely toothed. The leaf base is cordate. Fall color is an attractive yellow.

Overwintering buds are rather blunt and not sharp. The young twigs are light brown, lustrous, and slightly aromatic but less so than those of the sweet birch. The intermediate bark of the branches is silver or yellow with thin, papery layers separating and often curling at the edges, giving the trunk a ragged appearance. On large trees, the mature bark is made up of irregular, brown plates.

The flowers are in catkins. The male, or staminate, catkins are purplish and visible all winter, until they open in April or May. The female, or pistillate, catkins are greenish, erect, shorter, and thicker than those of the sweet birch and develop in the spring. Fruit is a cone with deciduous scales that matures in August or September.

The wood is heavy, strong, hard, and close-grained. The sapwood is light-colored, but the heartwood is dark red, which gives this wood the name of "red birch" to the lumber trade. The wood is used for flooring, woodenware, furniture, and other uses. It is prized as firewood.

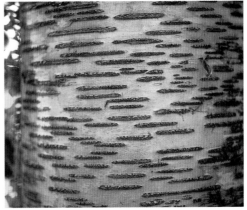

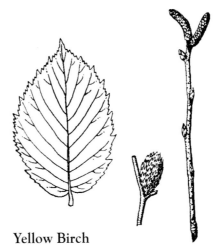

Yellow Birch

71

Sweet Birch

Sweet Birch—*Betula lenta*

The sweet birch is also known as black birch or cherry birch and occurs in the coves and deep ravine pockets of the sandstone and shale formations of eastern Ohio. Its range extends from Ashtabula County southward to Highland and Adams counties. It attains its best development on cool, northerly exposures and on rich slopes where it reaches an average height of 70 feet and a diameter of 2–3 feet. The tree is moderately slow growing but is of value for its protection to the soil in the rugged sandstone cliff areas of eastern Ohio. When found growing in Ohio, it is usually associated with the hemlock forest.

The bark of the trunk is dark brown, almost black, dull, and broken into large, irregular, but not papery, plates. The small branches and twigs are glossy with a uniform, brown color that looks to have been polished. The twigs are very aromatic. Twigs are cut and distilled for the production of birch oil that is used as wintergreen flavoring. Buds are somewhat pointed and sharp.

The leaves are simple and alternately borne. Leaves are oval to oblong and 3–4 inches (7½–10 cm) long. Foliage is dull and dark green on the upper leaf surface. Leaf margins are finely toothed. The upper leaf surface is glabrous with pubescent veins beneath. The leaf base is cordate.

The flowers are of two kinds. The male catkins are usually borne three to four on a shoot, form in the summer, and bloom the following April or May. Female catkins or "cones" open from mixed winter buds. The seeds ripen in late summer or autumn, and fall with the deciduous scales of the cone.

River Birch—*Betula nigra*

This is the only native birch found at lower elevations in the south. It is at home, as the name implies, along water courses and inhabits the deep, rich soils along the borders of streams, ponds, lakes, and swamps which are inundated for weeks at a time. In Ohio, it is limited to the southeastern portion of the state, extending from Fairfield County in a southeasterly fashion.

Young twigs are not aromatic when crushed. The bark provides a ready means for distinguishing this tree. Bark on 2–10-inch (5–25 cm) stems varies from tan to cinnamon-red in color and peels back in tough, papery layers. These layers persist on the trunk, presenting a very ragged and quite distinctive appearance. Unlike the bark of our other birches, the thin, papery layers are usually covered with a gray powder. On older trunks, the bark becomes thick, deeply furrowed, and reddish-brown in color.

The leaves are simple, alternate, and 2–3 inches (5–7½ cm) long. The upper leaf surface is dark green and the lower surface is a pale, yellow-green. Leaves are glaucous (bloomy) beneath with seven to nine pairs of veins. The leaf margin is more coarsely toothed than the sweet or yellow birches. The leaf base is wedge-shaped.

The flowers are two kinds of catkins growing on the same tree. Male catkin buds are conspicuous in the winter but open with the female catkins in April or May. The fruit is cone-shaped, about 1 inch (2½ cm) long, and densely crowded with little winged nutlets that ripen from May to June.

The wood is strong and fairly close-grained. It has been used in the manufacture of woodenware, in turnery, and for pulpwood. Since this tree is scattered in its distribution and mostly confined to banks of streams, it does not figure largely in commercial lumbering.

Recently, this tree has been heavily planted in Ohio's landscapes. All birch trees require acidic soil and are prone to developing an iron deficiency in alkaline soil regions. There is no practical control for the iron deficiency but to properly site this tree. Note that the natural range includes the acid soil regions of Ohio. A cultivar, 'Heritage,' was selected for unusually light bark color and is popular. River birch is resistant to the bronze birch borer.

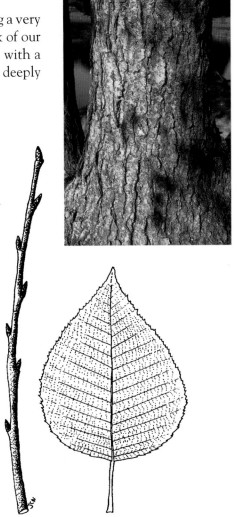

River Birch

73

European White Birch

European White Birch—
Betula pendula (verrucosa, alba)

A graceful tree, it is one of the most beautiful of the birches, planted quite extensively for lawn and ornamental purposes. Reaching heights of 40–60 feet with a wide, uniform crown, the European birch has slender, drooping branches. The European birch is not as well-adapted to Ohio landscapes as the native canoe or paper birch. Several horticultural types are planted including the cut-leaf cultivar (*Betula pendula* 'Gracilis') with fine, deeply cut leaves.

The trunk of the tree is short and rather stout. Bark is white on 2–10-inch (5–25 cm) stems and usually peels off in narrow, curly strips. The native canoe or paper birch has more colorful bark. Mature bark is deeply furrowed and almost black.

Leaves are 1–3 inches (2½–7½ cm) long with an acuminate leaf tip. Leaves are glabrous and dark green above and lighter beneath with three to seven pairs of veins per leaf. Foliage is more or less triangular in shape. The leaf base is wedge-shaped to truncate.

The bronze birch borer kills the European birch quickly in the landscape. Rarely does the European birch live more than five years in the landscape without an annual spray program. The paper birch has better bark color, but develops color one to two years later than European birch and commonly lives for 10–20 years without a spray program in Ohio. Because the bark colors later, the canoe, or paper, birch is less commonly grown in nurseries.

Carpinus — Hornbeam

Hornbeams are deciduous trees, usually with smooth, gray bark. Imbricate buds have many scales. Leaves are alternate and doubly toothed. Flowers are monoecious and borne in catkins. Fruit is a nutlet subtended on a bract.

Key to *Carpinus* Species

> I. Buds are usually of two distinct sizes and somewhat angled. Side veins of the leaves are unbranched and run straight to the teeth on the margins. Teeth at the ends of the veins are larger than the teeth between the veins. The bark of the trunk is a smooth, bluish-gray and covers the muscle-like ridges of the trunk. Trunks are usually twisted and fluted.
>
> *Carpinus caroliniana*—American Hornbeam

Description of Species

American Hornbeam (Blue-Beech)— *Carpinus caroliniana*

The American hornbeam is known also as musclewood, ironwood, and blue-beech. Blue-beech is a small, slow-growing, bushy tree with a spreading top of slender, crooked, or drooping branches. Hornbeam is found along streams and in low ground throughout the state as a forest understory tree. Its height is usually from 20–30 feet, and its trunk diameter is from 4–8 inches, although it sometimes grows larger.

American Hornbeam

The leaves of the hornbeam are simple, alternate, oval-shaped, and acute-tipped Leaves are 2–3 inches (5–7½ cm) in length. Side veins of the leaves are unbranched and run straight to the teeth on the margins. This characteristic separates American hornbeam from the hophornbeam that has similar foliage. Teeth at the ends of the veins are larger than the teeth between the veins. Leaf margins are doubly toothed. Foliage resembles that of the black or sweet birch, but is smaller.

Buds are usually of two distinct sizes and are somewhat angled. The smaller buds, at the terminal end, are vegetative buds. The larger, plumper buds further down the twig are mixed buds and contain both floral and leaf initials.

The trunk is fluted with irregular ridges extending up and down the tree. The bark is light gray to dark bluish-gray in color and sometimes marked with dark bands extending horizontally on the trunk. The tree is commonly multi-stemmed as a result of damage from the hornbeam borer that kills the tree to the soil line, where its stump sprouts and regenerates another tree.

The flowers are born in catkins. The male catkin is about 1½ inches (4 cm) long while the female is about ¾–1 inch (2–2½ cm) long. Female flowers have small, leaflike, three-lobed, green scales. The fruit is a nutlet about ⅓ inch (8 mm) long. When it falls, it is attached to the leaflike scale which acts as a wing and aids its distribution by the wind.

The wood is tough, close-grained, heavy, and strong. It is sometimes selected for use for levers, tool handles, wooden cogs, mallets, wedges, etc. The tree is of little commercial importance and often occupies space in the woods that should be utilized by more valuable kinds of trees if the trees are being grown for timber.

American Hornbeam

Ostrya — Hophornbeam

Hophornbeams are deciduous trees with scaly bark and scaly, pointed buds. Leaves are alternate and doubly toothed. Flowers are monoecious and borne in catkins. Fruit is a nutlet in a pendant, hop-like structure.

Key to *Ostrya* Species

I. Bud scales are marked with fine, longitudinal lines. Buds are not conspicuously variable in size or angle. Leaves with each side vein form one or two branches near the margin of the leaf. Teeth are of nearly the same size, making a uniformly toothed leaf margin. The bark of the trunk and main branches strips off in thin shreds.

Ostrya virginiana—American Hophornbeam (Ironwood)

Description of Species

American Hophornbeam (Ironwood)—*Ostrya virginiana*

The tree gets its common names from the qualities of its wood and the hop-like fruit. Hophornbeam is a small, slender, generally round-topped tree 30–40 feet high. Stems are 7–10 inches in diameter. The top consists of long, slender branches commonly drooping toward the ends. It is mostly found on dry soils throughout the upland regions. It normally exists as an understory tree, but is larger than the American hornbeam and likely to have a single stem.

The bark is mostly light brown or reddish-brown and finely divided into thin scales by which the tree can be recognized. Bud scales are marked with fine, longitudinal lines. Buds are not conspicuously variable in size or angled as in the American hornbeam.

The leaves are simple, alternate, and generally oblong in shape with narrowed tips. Leaves are from 2–3 inches (5–8 cm) long. Side veins of the leaves diverge into one or two branches near the margin of the leaf. Teeth are of nearly the same size, making a more uniformly toothed leaf margin than for hornbeam.

The flowers are monoecious. The male catkins form on the previous summer's twigs, while the female flowers are borne in erect catkins on the newly formed twigs. The fruit resembles that of the common hop vine and consists of a branch of leafy bracts 1–2 inches (2½–5 cm) long containing a number of flattened, ribbed nutlets.

The wood is strong, hard, and durable. Bark is light brown to white with thick, pale sapwood. It is often used for handles of tools, mallets, and other small articles. It is a good, small, ornamental tree near the lake in Ohio. The tree is intolerant of stressful urban sites in Ohio.

American Hophornbeam (Ironwood)

77

Fagus — Beech

Beeches are deciduous trees with long, scaly buds. Leaves are alternate with toothed to nearly entire leaf margins. Stipule scars are long and narrow. Stipules nearly meet around the stem. Flowers are monoecious. Fruit is a nut in a prickly bur.

Key to *Fagus* Species

I. Leaves are sharply and coarsely toothed with four to 14 pairs of veins. Leaves are 2½–4¼ inches (6–11 cm) long. Foliage color is dark bluish-green above and light green below. The bark of trunks and main branches is smooth and light gray.

Fagus grandiflora—American Beech

II. Leaves have wavy margins and are minutely toothed. Leaves have five to nine pairs of veins and are 2–4 inches (5–10 cm) long. Foliage color is glossy, dark green above and light green beneath. The ark of trunks and main branches is dark gray or brownish.

Fagus sylvatica—European Beech

American Beech

Description of *Fagus* Species
American Beech—
Fagus grandifolia (americana)

The American beech is native throughout the state. However, it makes its best growth in northeastern Ohio where is it conspicuously associated with the sugar maple. It is found widely scattered with oaks and hickories on rich, well-drained bottoms and glacial soils of southwestern and western Ohio. It is one of the most beautiful of all Ohio trees.

Leaves are sharply and coarsely toothed with four to 14 pairs of veins per leaf. Leaves are 2½–4¼ inches (6–11 cm) long and pointed at the

78

tip. Leaves are coarsely toothed along the margin. Mature leaves are almost leathery in texture. Foliage color is dark bluish-green above and light green below. Fall color is golden yellow to russet.

The winter buds are long, slender, pointed, and usually greater than ½ inch (13 mm) long. Stipule scars are long, narrow, and nearly encircle the stem. The bark is perhaps the most distinctive characteristic, as it maintains an unbroken, light gray surface throughout its life. So tempting is this smooth expanse to the owner of a jackknife that the beech has been well-designated the "initial tree," but this permanently disfigures the tree.

The flowers are monoecious and open in April or May. The small, brown, three-sided beech nuts are almost as well know as chestnuts. They usually form in pairs in a prickly bur. The kernel is sweet and edible but so small as to offer insufficient reward for the pains of biting open the thin shelled husk. The American beech flowers and fruits every several years and is a major source of food for wildlife during the mast years when the tree produces a good crop of seeds.

The wood of the beech is very hard and strong, although it will not last long on exposure to weather or in the soil. The tree is of economic importance. The wood is used for furniture, flooring, carpenters' tools, novelty wares, and rough framing lumber.

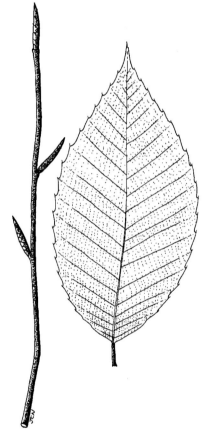

American Beech

79

European Beech

European Beech—*Fagus sylvatica*

The European beech is similar in appearance to our own native American beech, but the bark is less showy.

Greater tolerance of soil compaction characterizes the European beech. The European beech is preferred for landscape use because of its greater tolerance of human activity. Many named forms are available. European beech is slow to establish but grows rapidly once established.

Terminal buds are slightly smaller than the American beech but are still long and pointed. Terminal buds are less than ½ inch (13 mm) long. Stipule scars are long and narrow, and they nearly encircle the stem. Bark is a darker gray than the American beech and not as smooth or as attractive. The trunk supports stout, rugged branches with an upright tendency.

Leaves have wavy margins and are only minutely toothed. Leaves have five to nine pairs of veins and are 2–4 inches (5–10 cm) long. Foliage color is glossy, dark green above and light green beneath. Fall color is golden yellow to russet for the green-foliaged forms. Fall color is purple to brown for the purple-foliaged forms.

Several cultivars with purple summer-leaf color are planted for ornamental purposes. The leaves range in color from deep purplish-brown to a rich, bronze, metallic color. The cultivar *F. sylvatica* 'Riversii' is the one commonly planted for foliage color effect and is shown in the photograph above. A weeping type, *F. sylvatica* 'Pendula,' has dark green leaves and irregular branching, supporting a drooping or pendant top. The weeping type also occurs in a purple-leafed cultivar as well. A cut-leafed form is also available and is one of the most attractive selections.

Castanea — Chestnut

Chestnuts are deciduous trees with furrowed bark and scaly buds. Terminal buds are absent. Leaves are alternate and toothed with parallel veins. Flowers are monoecious and borne in catkins. Fruit is a nut in a prickly bur.

Key to *Castanea* Species

I. Leaves are glabrous and two to three times as long as wide. Leaves are from 4¼–9½ inches (11–24 cm) long. The leaf base is acute, or narrowed, toward the base. Leaves are coarsely toothed and have bristle-like tips. Buds and twigs are glabrous.

Castanea dentata—American Chestnut

II. Leaves are hairy beneath and 3¼–6 inches (8½–15 cm) long. Leaves are rounded, or square, at the base and are entirely or obscurely toothed along the margin. Buds and twigs are pubescent.

Castanea mollissima—Chinese Chestnut

Description of Species

American Chestnut—*Castanea dentata*

The chestnut was one of the most important trees in Ohio. It was entirely confined to the eastern portion of the state from Erie, southward to Franklin and Clermont counties. About the beginning of this century, it fell victim to chestnut blight, one of the most disastrous tree diseases. This canker disease was imported from Asia and has spread rapidly throughout New England and the Appalachian region. Occasionally, live sprouts may be found, but these usually canker and die back to the soil line when the trunk reaches 6 inches in diameter.

The long, pointed leaves have coarse teeth, each carrying a slender spine or bristle tip and are quite distinctive. Leaves are simple, alternate, and average 4¼–9½ inches (11–24 cm) long. Leaves are glabrous and two to three times as long as wide. Foliage is dark green in color. The leaf base is acute, or narrowed, toward the base. Its foliage makes it easy to distinguished it from the Chinese and European chestnuts.

American Chestnut

81

The showy male flowers are long, slender, whitish catkins opening in midsummer. The fruit is a prickly bur which opens at the first frost, or earlier, and drops two to three shiny, brown, sweet, edible nuts. These were harvested and sold earlier in this century.

Terminal buds are absent. Overwintering buds are ⅛–¼ inch (3–6 mm) long and ovoid in shape. Twigs and buds are brown and glabrous. Bark becomes broken into light gray, broad, flat ridges which often have a tendency toward a spiral course around the trunk.

The wood is light, soft, not strong, coarse-grained, and very durable in contact with the soil. These properties make the wood particularly valuable for posts, poles, and crossties as well as for light building construction. The wood is rich in tannin. The tree's wonderful sprouting ability had enabled it to reproduce prolifically after repeated cutting for railroad ties, poles, and other products.

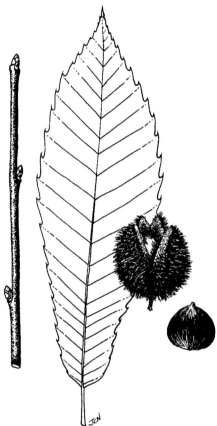

American Chestnut

Chinese Chestnut—
Castanea mollissima

Asiatic chestnuts from China and Japan have been introduced in recent years for reforestation and nut-culture purposes. Various hybrids of the Chinese chestnut (*Castanea mollissima*) have been developed with some resistance to chestnut blight but are not immune. Resistant selections include 'Jobson,' 'Carr,' 'Abundance,' 'Stoke,' 'Reliable,' and 'Yankee.'

The leaves of the Chinese chestnut are smaller than the native chestnut. Leaves are hairy beneath and 3¼–6 inches (8½–15 cm) long. The leaf base is more rounded and not as acute as the American chestnut. Leaf margins are serrate with bristle-like teeth.

Chinese Chestnut

Terminal buds are absent. Overwintering buds are ⅛–¼ inch (3–6 mm) long and ovoid in shape. Twigs and buds are brown and pubescent. Mature bark is grayish-brown and strongly furrowed.

The nuts are sweet and somewhat larger than the native chestnut but not as flavorful. At present, the form and type are inferior for lumber. The tree is branched lower to the ground and is smaller than the American chestnut. The Chinese chestnut rarely reaches 50 feet.

Quercus — Oaks

Oaks are deciduous or evergreen trees with scaly buds that are clustered at the ends of the twigs. Leaves are alternate with lobed, toothed, or entire margins. Flowers are monoecious. Male flowers are borne in catkins. Fruits are nuts (acorns). Evergreen forms are not cold-hardy in Ohio.

Key to *Quercus* Species

I. Leaves are lobed. Acorns take two years to mature: the red or black oak group. Overwintering buds are pointed.

    A. Lobes of the leaves end in bristles. Longest lobes are about as long as the central portion of the leaf is wide.

        1. Leaves are broadly obovate with three to five lobes mostly at the apex. Leaves are often rusty-woolly beneath. Foliage is 4–8 inches (10–20 cm) long and nearly as broad at the apex. Buds are reddish-brown and woolly. Twigs are usually dull.

            Quercus marilandica—Blackjack Oak

        11. Leaves are elliptic to oblong and not wider at the tip of the leaf.

           a. Deep green leaves are white to grayish-green and tomentose beneath. Foliage is 3–8 inches (7½–20 cm) long with three to seven narrow lobes that are often sickle-shaped. Twigs are rusty and woolly. Tree grows to 80 feet.

                Quercus falcata (rubra)—Southern Red (Spanish) Oak

          aa. Leaves and twigs are greenish below and not as elliptic or oblong.

            i. Buds are velvety tomentose (grayish and woolly) throughout and longer than ⅜ inches (9½ mm). Twigs are brown and shiny. Inner bark of twigs is yellowish-orange in color. Leaves are irregularly lobed halfway to the middle of the leaf blade or beyond. Foliage is 4–10 inches (10–25 cm) long.

                  Quercus velutina—Black Oak

            ii. Buds are not velvety tomentose. Winter buds and twigs are reddish. Inner bark of the twigs is not yellowish-orange.

                  Quercus rubra—Eastern Red Oak

    A) Longest lobes of the leaves are two to six times as long as the narrowest middle portion of the leaf blade. Leaves are glossy. Buds are ovate and less than ⅜ inch (9½ mm) long.

I) Leaves have conspicuous tufts of hair in the axils of the veins beneath. Tree is pyramidal with a straight, central stem when less than 12 inches (30½ cm) in diameter. Branches are open, slender, and horizontal in the center of the crown. Lower branches droop. Buds are light brown and glabrous, or only slightly hairy. Largest terminal buds are usually less than ¼ inch (6 mm) in length. Leaves are 3–5 inches (7½–13 cm) long and wedge-shaped at base.

Quercus palustris—Pin Oak

I I) Leaves have small, inconspicuous, axillary tufts of hairs in the axils of the veins beneath the leaf. Tree is broad-spreading with a round-topped and open head. Buds are dark reddish-brown and usually hairy above the middle of the bud. Largest terminal buds are usually ¼ inch (6 mm) or more in length. Leaves are 3–6 inches (8½–15 cm) long and nearly square at base.

Quercus coccinea—Scarlet Oak

AA) Longest lobes almost equal the widest middle part of the leaf. Leaves are dull. Buds are long, ovate, and slightly hairy. Leaves are 4¾–8¾ inches (12–22 cm) long, wedge-shaped at the base.

Quercus rubra—Eastern Red Oak

AA. Lobes are rounded and are without bristle-like points. Acorns mature in one year: the white oak group. Overwintering buds are rounded.
I. Twigs are glabrous or nearly so.
a. Leaves are glabrous, or only slightly hairy beneath. Petioles are more than ½ inch (13 mm) long. Leaves are usually wedge-shaped at the base. Foliage is 4–8 inches (10–20 cm) long. Buds are small and light brown in color with rounded tips. Twigs are slender, shiny, and purplish in color. Bark on the trunk and limbs is light in color and scaly.

Quercus alba—White Oak

aa. Leaves are woolly, or hairy, beneath. Leaves are coarsely toothed or shallowly lobed with six to eight pairs of lobes. Foliage is 4–6½ inches (10–16 cm) long. The outline of the leaf is oblong to obovate. Twigs are dull, yellowish-brown, and not hairy. Bark on older branches is light grayish and scaly, or curling away. Trees are heavily branched and twigs may have corky ridges.

Quercus bicolor—Swamp White Oak

I I. Twigs are plainly hairy or woolly.

           aa. Leaves are hairy and dull above. Foliage is deeply lobed throughout and 4–8 inches (10–20 cm) long. Twigs are reddish-brown. Buds are reddish-brown with rounded buds. Acorn cup is not fringed, or only slightly so.

Quercus stellata (minor)—Post Oak

II.   Leaves are not lobed.

  A. Leaves are toothed.

      I. Teeth of the leaves are sharp-pointed and coarse. Leaves are finely woolly beneath and 4–6½ inches (10–16½ cm) long. Foliage is dark or yellowish-green above. Largest terminal bud is less than ¼ inch (6 mm) long.

Quercus muhlenbergi—Yellow Chestnut (Chinquapin) Oak

      I I. Teeth of the leaves are blunt or rounded.

        a. Leaves are distinctly white, woolly beneath, and 4–6½ inches (10–16½ cm) long. Foliage is dark green above. Largest terminal buds are more than ¼ inch (6 mm) long. Bark is exfoliating and scaly on the older branches and trunk. Stem of the fruit is much longer than petiole of the leaf.

Quercus prinus (montana)—Chestnut Oak

  AA. Leaves are entire.

      I. Bud scales and leaves are glabrous beneath. Leaves are narrow, oblong, 2–4 inches (5–10 cm) long, and less than ½ inch (13 mm) wide. Foliage is glossy above and light green below.

Quercus phellos—Willow Oak

      I I. Bud scales and the undersides of the leaves are hairy. Leaves are oblong and 2¾–6½ inches (6–16½ cm) long and more than an inch (2½ cm) wide. Foliage is dark green above and pale green or brownish beneath.

Quercus imbricaria—Shingle Oak

Description of Species
White Oak—*Quercus alba*

The white oak is one of the most important timber trees. Its natural range includes almost the entire eastern half of the United States. It reaches a height of 60–100 feet with a diameter of 2–3 feet or more, and it sometimes becomes much larger. It is found in a wide variety of soils. When grown in a dense stand, it has a straight, continuous trunk, free of side branches for over half its height. In the open, however, the tree develops a broad crown with far-reaching limbs and will be wider than it is tall. Well-grown specimens are strikingly beautiful.

The leaves are alternate, simple, 4–8 inches (10–20 cm) long, and about half as broad. They are deeply divided into five to nine rounded, fingerlike lobes. Expanding leaves are soft and silvery gray, yellow, or red when unfolding. Mature leaves are bright green above and much paler below. Leaves are glabrous, or only slightly hairy beneath. Petioles are more than ½ inch (13 mm) long. Leaves are usually wedge-shaped at the base.

Buds are less than ¼ inch (6 mm) long and light brown in color, with rounded tips. Twigs are slender, shiny, and purplish in color. Twigs are glabrous and sometimes covered with a waxy bloom. The bark is thin and light ash gray with mature bark covered with loose scales or broad plates.

The fruit is an acorn which matures the first year. The elongate nut is ¾–1 inch (19–25 mm) long and light brown in color. About one-quarter of the acorn is enclosed in the warty cup. It is relished by hogs and other livestock. The acorns are a major source of food for wildlife such as deer and squirrels.

The wood is useful and valuable. It is heavy, strong, hard, close-grained, and durable. The color of the wood is light brown. The uses are many, including construction, shipbuilding, tight cooperage, furniture, implements, interior trim, flooring, and fuel. White oak is valuable for ornamental planting because of its urban-tolerance, storm resistance, and pest resistance. This tree is not commonly grown by nurseries since it is reported to be difficult to transplant and is rather slow-growing when small. Once established, the tree grows rapidly.

White Oak

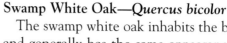

Swamp White Oak—*Quercus bicolor*

The swamp white oak inhabits the bottom or lowlands, and generally has the same appearance as the white oak when mature. When it is young, the swamp white oak has a more regular habit of growth. It is found in the flood plains and along streams in most areas of the state except the southeastern section where it is uncommon. The rounded habit of the young tree gives way to a massive, spreading, tree that may exceed 80 feet in height.

The mature bark is deeply and irregularly divided by fissures into broad ridges of a gray-brown color. Buds are rounded and about ⅛ inch (3 mm) long. Current year's twigs are a dull, yellowish-brown, and glabrous. Older twigs are light gray, scaly, and exfoliating. Twigs may be winged as is the bur oak. Trees are heavily branched, and twigs may have corky ridges. Intermediate bark is a light grayish-brown, fissured, and scaly.

Leaves are coarsely toothed or shallowly lobed with six to eight pairs of lobes. Foliage is 4–6 ½ inches (10–16 cm) long and 2–4 inches (5–10 cm) wide. The outline of the leaf is oblong to obovate. The leaves are generally broader at, or above, the middle of the leaf blade (pear-shaped). The base of the leaf is acute and/or wedge-shaped. The leaf margins are wavy and indented. Foliage color is dark green and shiny above and grayish beneath. Leaves are woolly or hairy beneath. The contrasting colors of the upper and lower leaf surfaces give rise to the species name (*bicolor*).

Flowers are monoecious and open in May. The acorn, or fruit, occurs commonly in pairs and, like all of the white oak group, requires only one season to mature. The nut is borne on slender stalks (peduncles) from 2–4 inches (5–10 cm) in length. The acorn is about 1 inch (2½ cm) long and ⅔ inch (17 mm) thick. It is enclosed for about one-third its length in a thick, unfringed cup.

The wood is heavy, hard, and strong. Lumber is used for similar purposes as the true white oak which includes furniture, cabinet work, flooring, cooperage, ties, fence posts, and fuel.

88

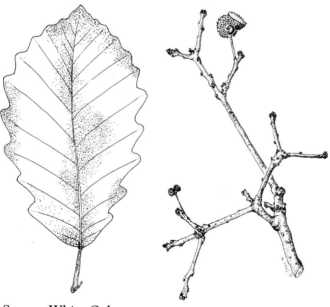

Swamp White Oak

Scarlet Oak—*Quercus coccinea*

Scarlet oak occurs abundantly on dry, rocky, and sandy soils throughout the uplands and ridges of southeastern Ohio. It is not common in other parts of the state. It usually reaches a height of 60–80 feet with a trunk diameter of 2–3 feet although sometimes larger. The branches droop at the ends and form a narrow, open crown.

The largest terminal buds are usually ¼ inch (6 mm) or more in length. The bark on young stems is smooth and light brown. On older trunks it is grayish-brown and divided into ridges. The mature bark is not as rough as that of the black oak. The bark is often mottled or spotted. Pointed buds are dark reddish-brown and usually hairy above the middle of the bud. Twigs are reddish and glossy. The inner bark is reddish.

The leaves are simple, alternate, 3–6 inches (7½–15 cm) long, 2½–4 inches (6–10 cm) wide, and nearly square at base. Leaves are usually oblong or oval and seven-lobed. The lobes are bristle-pointed and separated by round openings (sinuses) that extend two-thirds of the distance to the midrib, giving leaves a deeply "cut" appearance. Leaves have small, inconspicuous, axillary tufts of hairs in the axils of the veins beneath the leaf. The leaves turn a brilliant scarlet in the autumn and give the tree its common name.

The flowers are monoecious and appear when the leaves are one-half to two-thirds grown. Like other red oaks, the fruit takes two years to mature. The acorn is ½–1 inch (13–25 mm) long, reddish-brown, and often striped. When viewed from the end, the stripes on the acorn form small Cs at the point of the fruit. About one-half of the acorn is enclosed in the cup.

The wood is heavy, hard, strong, and coarse-grained. The lumber is sold as red oak and has the same uses. Scarlet oak is urban-tolerant and useful for ornamental planting but is reported to be difficult to transplant. It is uncommon in nurseries.

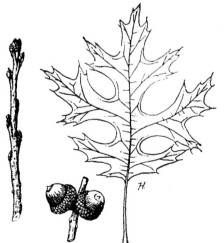

Scarlet Oak

89

Southern Red (Spanish) Oak— *Quercus falcata (rubra)*

The southern red oak is also commonly known as Spanish oak. Spanish oak usually grows to a height of 70–80 feet and a trunk diameter of 2–3 feet. Larger trees are not uncommon. It is one of the rarest of the native Ohio oaks and is found only in Scioto, Lawrence, and Jackson counties. Its large-spreading branches form a broad, round, open top.

Leaves are elliptic to oblong and not wider at the tip of the leaf as is the blackjack oak. Foliage is 3–8 inches (7½–20 cm) long with three to seven narrow lobes that are often sickle-shaped. The leaves are of two different types: (1) irregular-shaped lobes, mostly narrow and bristle-tipped with the central lobe often being the longest; or (2) pear-shaped with rounded and bristle-tipped lobes at the outer end. Foliage is dark, lustrous green above and whitish to grayish-green and tomentose beneath. The contrasting colors are strikingly seen in a wind or rain storm.

Twigs are reddish-brown and angled with pointed buds. A rusty-woolly pubescent may or may not be present. Overwintering buds are ¼ inch (6 mm) long, reddish-brown, and pubescent toward the tip. The bark is rough, though not deeply furrowed, and varies from light gray on younger trees to dark gray (almost black) on older ones. The bark is rich in tannin.

The flowers appear in April while the leaves are unfolding. The fruit ripens the second year. The small, rounded acorn is about ½ inch (13 mm) long and set in a thin, saucer-shaped cup which tapers to a short stem. This tree has an unusually small acorn. Heavy crops of seed occur every 3–5 years.

The wood is heavy, hard, coarse-grained, and less subject to defects than most other red oaks. It is used for rough lumber and for furniture, chairs, and tables. It is a desirable timber tree, especially on the poorer, drier soils.

Southern Red (Spanish) Oak

Shingle Oak—*Quercus imbricaria*

The shingle oak is found scattered over the entire state, usually growing as an individual. When growing alone, the tree develops a symmetrical, rounded crown. Young trees have drooping lower branches, lateral middle branches, and ascending upper branches. Young trees often retain the russet foliage through the winter and into spring when the old foliage is pushed off by the new foliage.

It forms a handsome tree. It is sometimes incorrectly called a "laurel" oak. The tree may exceed 80 feet in height. Shingle oak is one of the more commonly planted red oaks in Ohio. It is urban-tolerant and can be used as a street tree. The tendency to retain foliage during the winter, combined with the drooping lower branches allow this tree to serve as a large screen.

Foliage is unique among native red oaks as this tree has an entire leaf rather than the lobed margins more commonly seen. The alternate leaves are oblong in shape. Leaves are 2¾–6½ inches (7–16½ cm) long by 1–2 inches (3–5 cm) wide. Leaves are leathery in texture; shiny, dark green above; and pale green or brownish and pubescent below.

Twigs have the cluster buds that say oak. Twigs are greenish in color with small, pointed buds. Bud scales are hairy. The bark is thin and divided into broad, dark brown ridges by shallow fissures. Mature bark is similar to other red oaks and is dark gray and deeply furrowed.

The fruit is an acorn about ½ inch (13 mm) in length, borne singularly or in pairs. Acorns are rounded at the end, faintly streaked, and enclosed for about half of its length in a thin-walled cup. Like all members of the red oak group, the fruit requires two seasons to mature. This tree has an unusually small acorn. Heavy crops of seed occur every 3–5 years.

The wood is heavy, hard, and coarse-grained. It is used for common lumber, shingles (whence it got its common name), posts, and firewood. The tendency to retain lower branches makes this tree less valuable for lumber but the lumber is marketed as red oak.

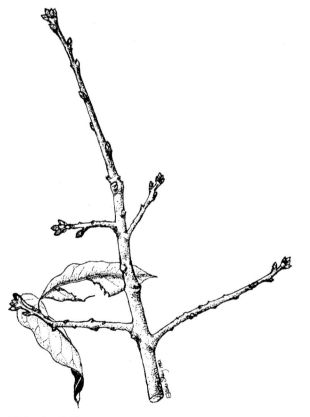

Shingle Oak

Bur (Mossycup) Oak—
Quercus macrocarpa

The bur oak occurs throughout the state, although it is chiefly confined to the central and western portions. In the eastern portion of Ohio it is rare and found only occasionally along streams in lowlands. It usually has a broad top of heavy, spreading branches and a relatively short body. At maturity, the tree attains a diameter of 5 feet or more and a height of over 80 feet.

Unlike other oaks, the bur oak is not often a part of the oak-hickory forest stand. It generally occurs in open stands (oak openings) and in fields. In fire-dominated landscapes such as oak openings, the bark is thick, deeply fissured, and quite fire resistant. The bur oak is more alkaline-soil-tolerant than many other oaks.

The leaves resemble those of the common white oak and have rounded lobes. Bur oak differs in that it has a pair of deep sinuses toward the base and wavy notches on the broad, middle, and upper portions of the leaf. Leaves are said to be fiddle-shaped. They range from 6–9½ inches (15–24 cm) long and 3–6 inches (7½–15 cm) wide. Leaves are glabrous and shiny with a deep green color on the upper leaf surface.

Twigs are pubescent and gray or yellowish-brown in color. Two-year and older twigs are often winged. Rounded buds are less than ¼ inch (6 mm) in length, rounded in outline, and often flattened against the twig. The mature bark is light gray, usually broken up into small, narrow flakes, and is thinner when fire is not a factor.

Bur oak takes its name from the fringe around the cup of the acorn. The fruit, or acorn, is deeply set in a fringed cup. These acorns are the largest of the oaks and are sometimes 1 inch (25 mm) or more in diameter. Acorns do vary widely in size and the degree to which the nut is enclosed in the mossy fringed cup. Heavy crops of seed occur every 3–5 years and are a major food source for deer and other wildlife when abundant.

The wood is heavy, hard, strong, and durable. It is used for much the same purposes as the other white oaks, including lumber, crossties, and fuel.

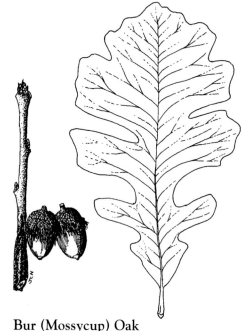

Bur (Mossycup) Oak

92

Blackjack Oak—*Quercus marilandica*

The occurrence of blackjack oak is said to indicate poor soil. It is certain that blackjack oak often occurs on dry, or poorly drained, gravel, clay, or sandy, upland soils where few other forest trees thrive. This may account for the tree's slow rate of growth. It is found locally in the extreme southeastern part of the state, usually on sharp ridges where it is associated with scrub pine, scarlet oaks, and chestnut oaks.

The tree sometimes reaches heights of 50–60 feet and a trunk diameter of 16 inches, but it is usually much smaller. Blackjack oak's hard, stiff, drooping branches form a dense crown which usually contains many persistent, dead twigs.

Blackjack Oak

The bristle-tipped leaves have a leathery texture. They are dark green on the upper surface and lighter beneath. Leaves are broadly obovate with three to five lobes, mostly at the apex. Leaves are often rusty-woolly beneath. Foliage is 4–8 inches (10–20 cm) long and nearly as broad at the apex.

The pointed overwintering buds are borne in clusters and are ¼–⅓ inch (6–8 mm) long. Buds are reddish-brown and woolly. Twigs are usually dull, reddish-brown, becoming ash gray. The bark is rough, very dark (often nearly black), and broken into small, hard scales, or flakes.

Flowers are monoecious and open in May. The fruit is an acorn about ¾ inch (19 mm) long, yellowish-brown in color, and often striped. The acorn is enclosed for at least half its length in a thick, light brown cup. Acorns take two years to mature.

The wood is heavy, hard, and strong but not commonly used in commerce because of its small size and branchy crown. When the wood is used at all, it is used mostly for firewood and mine props.

Chinquapin Oak (Yellow Oak)—
Quercus muhlenbergi

This oak is an excellent timber tree and occurs throughout the state, but it is more abundant in the southwestern portion. It grows on practically all classes of soil and in all moisture conditions except swamps, and is a very tenacious tree on shallow, dry soil. This tree is an indicator of alkaline soils. It reaches heights of 70–90 feet and is one of the largest oaks native to Ohio. The straight, shapely trunk bears a round-topped head composed of small branches, which makes it an attractive shade tree. The nursery industry rarely offers this tree, in part because it is reported to be difficult to transplant.

The leaves are oblong, 4–6½ inches (10–16½ cm) in length and 1½–3 inches (4–7½ cm) wide. The leaf margins are regularly toothed or notched and frequently have glandular tips. The teeth are more acute-tipped and are more American chestnut-like than chestnut oak. Leaves are dark green above and whitish beneath.

Chinquapin Oak

The foliage texture is finer than most other oaks. Leaves are not lobed, as are most oaks.

The largest terminal bud is less than ¼ inch (6 mm) long. Buds are generally rounded and a pale brown color. Twigs are slender, rounded, and glabrous. The mature bark is light gray and breaks up into short, narrow flakes on the main trunk and older limbs.

Chinquapin oak has monoecious flowers. The fruit ripens in the fall of the first season and is light to dark brown when ripe and edible if roasted. This acorn is from ½–1 inch (13–25 mm) long, usually not as wide, and set in a shallow cup. This is one of the smallest acorns of our native white oaks. The seed is very attractive to wildlife who readily harvest it. It is difficult to beat the wildlife to the seed and therefore this desirable tree is rarely found in nurseries.

The wood is heavy, very hard, strong, durable, and takes an excellent polish. It is used for timbers, crossties, fence posts, fuel, and furniture.

Pin Oak—*Quercus palustris*

Pin oak is found naturally on the rich, moist soil of bottom lands and borders of swamps. While not common on a statewide basis, it is often found growing in pure stands on wet, heavy, clay soils. The pin oak "flats" of Brown, Clermont, Warren, and Hamilton counties in southwestern Ohio are examples of local abundance.

Pin oaks commonly attain heights of 50–70 feet with trunk diameters up to 2 feet or more. The tree normally has a single, upright stem with numerous long, tough branches. The many small, bristling twigs and branches give the tree its name.

Fall color ranges from russet to orange and may be showy. Because of its beauty, hardiness, urban-tolerance, and fairly rapid growth, the pin oak makes a good ornamental tree. Care must be taken to plant trees that are from locally adapted seed sources. Native pin oaks are adapted to Ohio's

Chinquapin Oak

94

neutral soils and rarely show an iron deficiency. Iron deficiencies are common on seedlings from areas such as Tennessee where the parent trees are adapted to acid soils.

Pin oak has a pyramidal habit with a straight, central stem when less than 12 inches (30½ cm) in diameter. Lower branches droop, the middle branches are lateral, and the upper branches ascend. Older trees have the typical habit of the red oak group and broaden with age to become as broad as they are tall.

The leaves generally resemble those of scarlet oak, except their rounded openings do not extend so near to the midrib, and their size is somewhat smaller. Leaves are 3–5 inches (7½–12 cm) long and 2–4 inches (5–10 cm) wide. Leaves are glossy, deep green above and light green beneath. Leaves have conspicuous tufts of hair in the axils of the veins beneath. The leaf base is wedge-shaped.

Buds are not velvety tomentose, but are light brown and glabrous, or only slightly hairy. The largest terminal buds are usually less than ¼ inch (6 mm) in length. Winter buds and twigs are reddish with greenish inner bark. The bark on young trees is smooth, shiny and light brown. On old trunks bark is light grayish-brown, fissured, and covered by small, close scales.

The monoecious flowers appear when the leaves are about one-third grown. The female flowers take two years to mature into an acorn. Male catkins are borne on the same tree. The fruit is a hemispherical acorn, about ½ inch (13 mm) long. The acorn is light brown in color, often striped, and enclosed at the base in a thin, shallow, saucer-shaped cup. This tree has an unusually small acorn. Heavy crops of seed occur every 3–5 years.

The wood is heavy, hard, strong, and usually knotty. It is light brown with thin, darker-colored sapwood. It is sold for the same uses as other red oaks, but is generally not as good in quality due to the tendency to retain the lower branches.

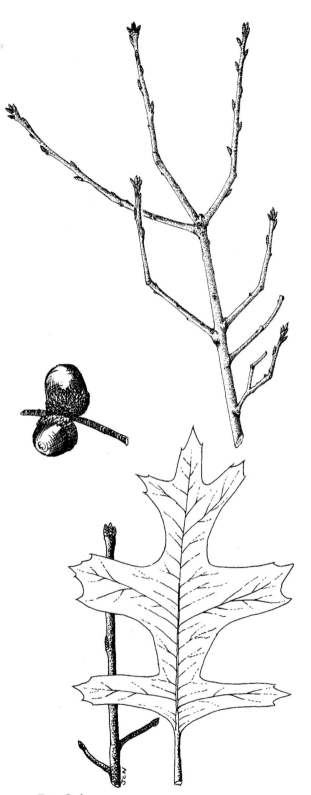

Pin Oak

95

Willow Oak—*Quercus phellos*

Willow oak is a tree that reaches 80 feet in height and is quite similar to its relative, the native shingle oak (*Quercus imbricaria*). It is reported locally in Jackson and Scioto counties but may be escaped in those counties. The native range is southward, where it is common in Kentucky and Tennessee. It is found not only in lowlands and along borders of rivers and swamps but also on rich, sandy uplands.

It is a beautiful, long-lived tree and is much desired for roadsides, lawns, and park plantings. It is the most common shade tree in the middle South and gives way to the live oak in the deep South.

Leaves are entire and quite different than most oaks. The leaves of the willow oak are narrower and more willowlike than the shingle oak. The slender willowlike leaves on a tree whose growth habit is manifestly that of a red oak make the tree easy to identify. The leaves are 2–4 inches (5–10 cm) long and ½–¾ inch (13–19 mm) wide with smooth or slightly wavy margins. Like other red oaks, the end of the leaf is bristle-tipped. Leaves are

Willow Oak

glabrous, shiny, light green above and dull below, and the leaf arrangement is alternate.

Twigs are fine-textured and have small, pointed buds less than ¼ inch (6 mm) long. The imbricate buds are glabrous. Twigs are reddish-brown in color when young. The bark generally remains smooth for a number of years, becoming gray in color. With age, the bark becomes slightly roughened and divided by narrow ridges.

The small acorns are closely set along the stem, and mature at the end of the second year. The nut is a light brown hemisphere about ½ inch (13 mm) in diameter with its base scarcely enclosed in the shallow, reddish-brown cup. The fruit is small when compared to most other oaks. The nuts are eaten by blue jays, grackles (blackbirds), and several other species of birds, as well as by rodents. Oaks generally bear fruit heavily every 3–5 years and lightly, or not at all, in other years.

The wood is not separated commercially from other species in the red oak group. It is heavy, strong, rather coarse-grained, light brown tinged with red, and not durable when exposed to the weather. It is used locally for crossties, bridges, planks, barn sills, and general construction.

Chestnut Oak—*Quercus prinus (montana)*

Chestnut oak is also known as mountain oak and rock oak because its leaf resembles that of the chestnut and because of its fondness for rocky mountain ridges. It is found widely distributed in the hilly areas of southern and eastern Ohio, on dry, rocky slopes and ridges. It is uncommonly found in rich mesic sites, but where it is found, it looks like another, more massive tree.

On poor sites it is a spreading tree reaching 30–50 feet. Its trunk frequently divides into several large, angular limbs making an open, irregular-shaped head. On good sites, the chestnut oak becomes a massive tree, growing to 80 feet in height with a spreading crown somewhat like the white oak. In 1997, the largest chestnut oak in Ohio was almost 5 feet in diameter (trunk), 129 feet in height, and 110 feet across.

The leaves are 4–6½ inches (10–16½ cm) long, simple, and alternate. Leaf shape is oblong, rounded at the tip, and irregularly scalloped, or wavy, on the margin (not sharp-toothed as in chinquapin oak). Foliage is normally widest, at or above, the middle of the leaf. Foliage is a shiny, yellowish-green color above and lighter green, white, and woolly beneath.

Twigs are glabrous. Buds are acute-tipped and large (¼ inch [6 mm] long or longer). Buds are slightly pubescent, or ciliate, above the middle of the bud. The bark is dark, reddish-brown, thick, and deeply divided into broad, rounded ridges on older trees.

The May flowers are monoecious and similar to those of the white oak. The fruit is an acorn about an inch (25 mm) long, oval, shiny brown and enclosed to half its length in a cup. The acorn is longer than it is wide. It ripens in one season, and like the acorn of the white oak, sprouts in the autumn soon after falling to the ground. The cup is thin, deep, and hairy inside.

The wood is generally similar to that of the other upland white oaks which is heavy, hard, strong, and durable, especially in contact with the soil. It is extensively cut into crossties and heavy timbers for bridges, railroad tracks, and other rough construction. It is also used for fence posts and fuel.

Chestnut Oak

Eastern Red Oak—*Quercus rubra (borealis)*

The eastern red oak occurs throughout the state, but is more abundant and of better quality in the heavy, clay soils of the northwest, central, and northeast portions of the state. It is of mesic sites and not found in swamps. It normally attains a height of about 70 feet with a diameter of 2–3 feet, but is sometimes much larger. The forest-grown tree is tall and straight with a clear trunk and narrow crown.

The simple, alternate, leaves are 4¾–8¾ inches (12–22 cm) long, 4–6 inches (10–15 cm) wide, wedge-shaped at the base, and lobed about halfway to the middle. The leaf is broader above the middle of the leaf blade. The blade is divided into seven to nine lobes (each lobe being somewhat coarsely toothed and bristle-tipped). Leaves are dull green above and paler below. Fall color ranges from a russet to a brilliant red.

Twigs are shiny and reddish, as the name suggests, in the winter. Reddish buds are clustered, ¼ inch (6 mm) long, ovate, and slightly hairy. The bark on young stems is smooth and from gray to green in color. Mature bark is thick, gray, and broken by shallow fissures into regular, flat, smooth-surfaced plates on older trees. Unfissured patches of bark are common on the mature bark of Eastern red oak.

The flowers, as in all the oaks, are monoecious. The male is long, drooping, clustered catkins opening with the leaves. The female flowers are solitary or slightly clustered. The fruit is a large acorn that matures the second year. The nut is globose and from ¾–1¼ inches (19–32 mm) long with blunt tips and a flat base. Only the base of the acorn is enclosed in the shallow, dark brown cup.

The wood is hard, strong, and coarse-grained with light reddish-brown heartwood and thin, lighter-colored sapwood. It is used for interior finishes, construction, furniture, and crossties. Because of its rapid growth, high-grade wood, and relative freedom from insect and disease attack, it is widely planted as a shade tree.

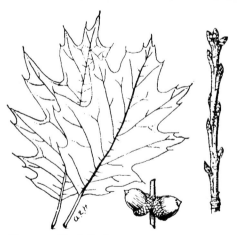

Eastern Red Oak

98

Post Oak—*Quercus stellata (minor)*

The post oak is usually a medium-sized tree with a rounded crown commonly reaching a height of 40–60 feet and a diameter of 1–2 feet. Sometimes post oaks grow considerably larger. Poor soils are favored by this tree. It occurs most abundantly in southeastern Ohio from Franklin and Madison counties southward and eastward. This tree is commonly used as a landscape tree in Texas where the drought- and urban-tolerance is desired. The moderate size should make it more popular in Ohio in the future.

Buds are reddish-brown and rounded. The stout, young twigs and leaves are coated at first with a thick, light-colored fuzz, which soon becomes darker and drops away entirely. Twigs and buds are reddish-brown in color.

The leaves are usually 4–8 inches (10–20 cm) long and nearly as broad. Rounded lobes have deep sinuses and are broadest at the ends of the lobes. The outline of the leaf is somewhat cross-shaped. Foliage is thick and leathery. Leaves are shiny and dark green on the upper surface, but lighter green, rough, and pubescent beneath.

The flowers, like those of the other oaks, are monoecious. The male flowers are borne in drooping, clustered catkins. Female flowers are inconspicuous. The fruit is an oval acorn, ½–1 inch (13–25 mm) long, and set in a small cup which may or may not be stalked. Fruit matures in a single season and is not fringed.

The bark is rougher and darker than that of other white oaks and broken into smaller scales. The wood is very heavy, hard, close-grained, light to dark brown, and durable in contact with the soil. It is used for crossties, fence posts, furniture, and other purposes similar to other oaks of the white oak group.

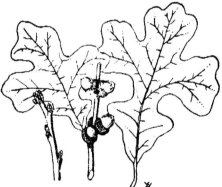

Post Oak

99

Black Oak—*Quercus velutina*

The black oaks grow to about 80 feet in height and 2–3 feet in diameter and is a typical red- or black-oak-group tree. The large crowns are irregularly shaped and wide with a clear trunk for 20 feet or more. Its growth is rather slow. It is commonly found on dry plains and ridges. Unlike the closely related red oak, the black oak is rarely seen on rich ground. Along the old glacial shorelines in northwestern Ohio, it occurs in nearly pure stands from Lucas County westward to the Indiana line.

The leaves are alternate, simple, 4–10 inches (10–25 cm) long and 3–8 inches (7½–20 cm) wide. Leaves may be shallowly or deeply lobed. The shape varies greatly. Leaves are similar to the red oak but are generally larger and not as deeply lobed. Lobes are bristle-tipped. When mature, the leaves are dark, shiny, and green on the upper surface and pale on the underside of the leaf. The lower leaf surface is covered with conspicuous, rusty brown hairs in the forks of the veins.

Buds are velvety tomentose (grayish-woolly) throughout and longer than ⅜ inches (9½ cm) long. Twigs are brown and shiny. Inner bark of twigs is yellowish-orange in color. The bark on the very young trunk is smooth and dark brown. The bright yellow color and bitter taste of the inner bark is due to the tannic acid content of the bark and is a distinguishing characteristic. Mature bark becomes thick and black with deep furrows and rough, broken ridges.

Black Oak

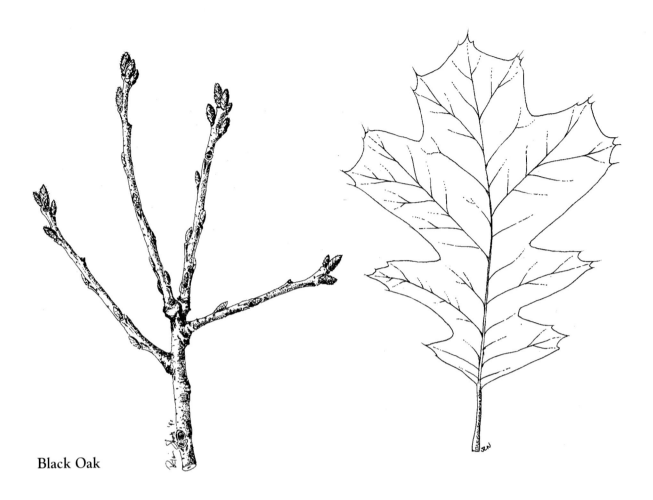

Black Oak

Flowers are monoecious and open in May. The light brown nut is large (¾–1 inch [19–25 mm] long) and hemispherical in shape. From one-half to three-quarters of the nut is enclosed in the thin, dark brown, scaly cup. The kernel is yellow and extremely bitter. The fruit matures the second season.

The wood is hard, heavy, strong, and coarse-grained. The wood checks, or cracks, easily as it dries. Lumber is a bright reddish-brown with a thin, outer edge of paler sapwood. Black oak is used for the same purposes as red oak under whose name it is marketed.

Ulmus — Elm

Elms are deciduous trees with scaly (imbricate) buds. Leaves are arranged in an alternate fashion. Leaf margins are doubly toothed and often meet in an oblique pattern at the base of the leaf. Flowers are perfect and have both functional male and female parts. The fruit is a samara (winged nutlet).

Key to *Ulmus* Species

I. Older twigs are corky.

    A.   Buds are pubescent (hairy) and sharply pointed. Leaves are 2–4 inches (5–10 cm) long without a hairy margin. Branches have irregular, corky wings. This tree is a large plant growing to 100 feet.

Ulmus thomasi (racemosa)—Rock (Cork) Elm

    AA. Buds are glabrous and smaller than those of rock elm. Leaves are 1¼–2¼ inches (3–5¾ cm) long with minutely, hairy margins. Branches usually have two corky wings opposite each other on the stem. Tree is smaller and reaches 50 feet in height.

Ulmus alata—Winged Elm

II. Older twigs are seldom corky.

    A.   Leaves are small, narrow, and less than 3 inches (7½ cm) long.

        I. Bark is rough and ridged. Leaves are 1–3 inches (2½–7½ cm) long and dark green. Leaves are smooth above and glabrous beneath. Flowers appear in the spring. This tree is often incorrectly offered in the trade as Chinese Elm.

Ulmus pumila—Siberian Elm

        II. Bark is smooth or flaky. Leaves are ¾–2 inches (2–5 cm) long. Young leaves are pubescent (hairy) beneath and glossy above. Foliage is somewhat leathery at maturity. This tree flowers in the fall.

Ulmus parvifolia—Lacebark Elm

    AA. Leaves are more than 3 inches (7½ cm) long and broader than the previous trees.

        I. Leaves are broadest above the middle, rough to the touch above, and pubescent (hairy) beneath. Foliage is abruptly pointed and tends to develop three points instead of one. Leaves are short-petioled and 3¼–6½ inches (8½–16½ cm) long. Branches are reddish-brown in color and hairy when young.

Ulmus glabra—Scotch Elm

11. Leaves are broadest at or below the middle and taper forward to a single point or tip.
   a. One-year-old twigs are rough, grayish, and lighter in color than the buds which are pubescent and rusty-brown to black. Flower buds are conspicuous in the winter. Winter buds are globose, reddish-orange in color, and hairy at the tip. Leaves are 4–8 inches (10–20 cm) long, rough above, and densely hairy beneath.

   Ulmus rubra (fulva)—Slippery Elm

   aa. One-year-old twigs are not rough, although they are often hairy. Buds and twigs are more uniformly brownish. Leaves are less pointed and not as decidedly roughened as the slippery elm.
      i. One-year-old twigs are glabrous near maturity but are often pubescent when young. Leaves are 4–6 inches (10–15 cm) long. Foliage is glabrous and rough above but hairy to nearly glabrous below.

      Ulmus americana—American Elm

      ii. One-year-old twigs are very hairy. Leaves are 2–3¼ inches (5–8½ cm) long, dark green, rough above, and soft and hairy below. Bark is dark and deeply ridged. Tree suckers freely.

      Ulmus procera (campestris)—English Elm

Description of Species
Winged Elm—*Ulmus alata*

The winged elm gets its common name from the thin, corky ridges, or wings, usually found on the smaller branches. Generally, winged elms are scattered over the southern Ohio counties. The tree grows rapidly, but rarely exceeds 2 feet in trunk diameter and 50 feet in height. It forms a rather open, round-topped head. This native American elm is sensitive to Dutch elm disease and elm yellows but is somewhat resistant to elm-leaf beetle, as are the other native American elms.

The leaves are simple, alternate, 1¼–2¼ inches (3–5¾ cm) long, and half as wide. The foliage is smaller than those of any other elm native to Ohio. The leaf margin is coarsely and doubly serrate and minutely hairy. Foliage is thick, dark green, and smooth above and pale and softly downy below.

Terminal buds are absent. Imbricate buds are reddish-brown, glabrous, and smaller than those of American elm. The bark is light brown tinged with red, and divided into irregular, flat ridges and fissures. Branches usually have two corky wings opposite each other on the stem.

The flowers appear in early spring long before the leaves unfold. The fruit ripens in the spring about the time the leaves appear. The fruit is winged; tipped with two small, incurved awns or beaks; oblong; and reddish-brown in color. Samaras are ⅓ inch (8 mm) long with long, slender stalks at the base covered with white hairs.

The wood of the winged elm is very similar to other elms: heavy, hard, strong, and difficult to split. Rope made of the inner bark was used for binding and wrapping purposes.

103

American (White) Elm—
Ulmus americana

This is the famous shade tree of New England whose range extends to the Rocky Mountains and southward to Texas. It is common in this vast area except in the high mountains and wet bottom lands. It reaches an average height of 50–70 feet and a trunk diameter of 4–5 feet. Almost every fence row in Ohio contains some American elm. Because of its spreading, fan-shaped form and graceful, pendulous branches, the American elm justly holds its place as one of the United States' most beautiful trees.

The leaves are alternate, simple, 4–6 inches (10–15 cm) long, rather thick, and with an uneven leaf base. Foliage is glabrous and rough above but hairy to nearly glabrous below. Leaves are less pointed and not so decidedly roughened as slippery elm. Leaf margins are doubly toothed. The leaf veins are very pronounced and run in parallel lines from the midrib to leaf edge.

Terminal buds are absent. One-year-old twigs are glabrous near maturity, but are often pubescent (hairy) when young. One-year-old twigs are not rough, although they are often hairy. Buds and twigs are uniformly brownish in color.

The bark is dark gray; divided into irregular, flat-topped, thick ridges; and is generally firm, though on old trees it tends

American (White) Elm

to come off in flakes. An incision in the bark ridge will show alternate layers of brown and white that some refer to as "Oreo bark". The bark is an excellent identification feature.

The greenish flowers are small, perfect, and borne on slender stalks, sometimes an inch (25 mm) long. Flowers appear before the leaves in very early spring. The fruit is a light green, oval-shaped samara (winged fruit) with the seed portion in the center and surrounded entirely by a wing. A deep notch in the end of the wing is distinctive of the species. The seed ripens in the spring and is widely disseminated by the wind.

The wood is heavy, hard, strong, tough, and difficult to split. It is used for paneling, rough construction, and veneer for baskets and crates. Like other American elms, the true American elm is susceptible to the Dutch Elm disease and phloem necrosis (elm yellows) but somewhat resistant to elm-leaf beetle feeding.

During the '20s and '30s, American elm was planted almost to the exclusion of other trees, due to the incredible urban-tolerance of *Ulmus americana*. The lack of diversity set U.S. cities up for the introduction of Dutch elm disease (DED) from Europe. The introduction of the exotic disease, an efficient insect carrier, and a monoculture of susceptible trees allowed this disease to spread rapidly. Many cities now ban American elm from city plantings. This is unfortunate, since urban stress is more of a threat to city trees than DED is a threat to American elm. We could increase the service life of city trees by planting sensitive American elms in limited numbers, especially in stressful sites. The really good news is that three DED-tolerant American elms have been introduced since 1990. 'New Harmony,' 'Princeton,' and 'Valley Forge' are now finding their way into our cities and should again grace our city streets while reducing the impact of DED. American elm is still sensitive to phloem necrosis (elm yellows), but this disease is generally not severe in Ohio.

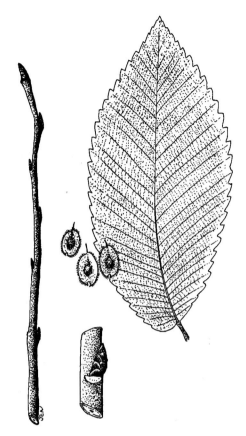

American (White) Elm

Slippery (Red) Elm—*Ulmus rubra (fulva)*

The slippery elm, or red elm, grows in all sections of the state, but is nowhere abundant. It is found principally on the banks of streams and on low hillsides in rich soils. It is a tree of small to moderate size, but not as vase-shaped as the American elm. It is usually less than 60 feet in height and 16 inches in trunk diameter, although trees of larger dimensions are occasionally found. This red elm is sensitive to Dutch elm disease and elm yellows but is somewhat resistant to elm-leaf beetle, as are the other American elms.

The thick leaves are simple, alternate, and have unsymmetrical leaf bases. Leaves are 4–8 inches (10–20 cm) long, rough above, and densely hairy beneath. Leaves are broadest at or below the middle, and taper forward to a single point or tip. Leaf margins are doubly toothed. Color of the foliage is dark green and the leaves are rough on both sides.

Terminal buds are absent. One-year-old twigs are rough, grayish, and without wings. Twigs are lighter-colored than the pubescent buds which are rusty to nearly black in color. Flower buds are conspicuous in the winter. Winter buds are globose, reddish-orange in color, and hairy at the tip.

The bark on the trunk is usually 1 inch (25 mm) thick, dark grayish-brown, and broken into flat ridges by shallow fissures. The inner bark is used to some extent for medicinal purposes, as it is fragrant and when chewed, affords a slippery, mucilaginous substance. The tree gets it name from the slippery substance.

Flower buds are plump, reddish or orange in color, and hairy at the apex. The flowers appear in early spring, and the fruit ripens when the leaves are about half grown. The fruit consists of a seed surrounded by a thin, broad, greenish wing about ½ inch (13 mm) in diameter. The wood is close-grained, tough, strong, heavy, and hard.

Slippery (Red) Elm

106

Scotch (Wych) Elm—*Ulmus glabra*

Scotch elm is a native of Europe and planted for ornamental purposes. The standard tree has a broad crown with upright branches. One cultivar, the 'Camperdown' elm, is commonly planted for its weeping habit and is often budded on a Siberian elm understock. European elms are sensitive to Dutch elm disease and elm yellows, as are the American elms. American elms are more resistant to the elm-leaf beetle than Scotch elm.

Terminal buds are absent. Buds are imbricate and ¼ inch (6 mm) long. Branches are reddish-brown in color and hairy when young. Bark on the main stem and branches is prominently smooth and without scales or corky ridges.

Leaves are short-petioled, 3¼–6½ inches (8½–16½ cm) long, and nearly as wide. Leaves are broadest above the middle, rough to the touch above, and pubescent beneath. Foliage is abruptly pointed and tends to develop three points instead of one. Leaves are dark green in color and tend to persist into late fall.

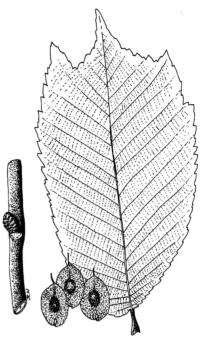

Scotch (Wych) Elm

Lacebark Elm—*Ulmus parvifolia*

Lacebark elm is a medium-sized tree that grows to 60 feet or more. The tree may have a vase-shaped habit or an upright, oval one. Many people prefer the vase-shaped habit, but the upright, oval habit is more storm resistant. The original common name was Chinese elm and was usually confused with Siberian elm. To avoid confusion, the name lacebark elm is now preferred. Lacebark elm is tolerant of Dutch elm disease, elm yellows, and elm-leaf beetle. The true Chinese elm (*U. parvifolia*) develops into a better tree for ornamental plantings than the Siberian elm. Elms are very urban-tolerant, and the lacebark elm is no exception.

Leaves of this elm are the smallest of the elms as the scientific name suggests. Leaves are a dark, glossy green and range from ¾–2 inches (2–5 cm) long. Young leaves are pubescent beneath and glossy above. Foliage is somewhat leathery at maturity. Leaves have serrate, rather than doubly serrate, leaf margins. Leaf bases are uneven. Fall color ranges from yellow to purple and is unusually good when compared to other elms.

Terminal buds are absent. Lateral buds are less than ⅛ inch (3 mm) long and are the smallest of the elms. Twigs are very fine-textured as well. Bark is gray for young bark. Intermediate bark may exfoliate into green, orange, and gray plates. The exfoliating bark gives rise to the preferred common name.

Lacebark Elm

Since flowers open in August and September, late-flowering easily separates this tree from the spring-flowering elms, such as Siberian elm, that are similar in many respects. As it matures, the winged samara is often reddish and showy against the dark foliage. Fruit matures in October and November. Fruiting time separates lacebark elm from Siberian elm as well. Most elms have conspicuous, rounded floral buds during the winter, but lacebark elm does not since it flowers in the fall and flower buds form in the summer.

Lacebark Elm

This tree was introduced from Korea, Japan, and China. The large native area ranges from places where it is nearly frost-free to areas that are colder than parts of Ohio. This tree was used in southern California and sold as evergreen elm. Not surprisingly, these selections are not hardy in Ohio. Care must be taken to ensure that cold-hardy seed sources are used. 'Ohio,' 'Dynasty,' and 'Pathfinder' are clones that have proven cold-tolerance. This tree is an excellent ornamental for Ohio gardens because of its glossy foliage, fall color, attractive bark, resistance to elm-leaf beetle, and disease-tolerance.

English Elm—*Ulmus procera (campestris)*

This is a large tree native of England and Europe. It reaches heights of 60–80 feet. Like most elms, it is urban-tolerant. English elm grows in an upright, oval configuration. This is quite different than the habit of the native American elm with its vase shape. The state champion English elm is on the Columbus campus of The Ohio State University and is 100 feet high and 70 feet across. European elms are as sensi-

English Elm

Cel

Ha
are sr
Unise

Key

Desc
Hack
Th
founc
north
abunc
rich, :
Ohio
of soi
dium-
10–2(
open,
an olc
as a y(
ten cr
is mac
bristl
excell
urban
Th
again!

tive to Dutch elm disease and elm yellows as are the American elms, though the American elms are more resistant to the elm-leaf beetle than English elm. The English elm suckers freely.

The leaves are dark green and remain on the tree late into the fall. Growing only 2–3¼ inches (5–8½ cm) in length, the foliage is smaller than many other elms. Leaves are dark green and rough above but soft and hairy below.

Terminal buds are absent. One-year-old twigs are very hairy. Bark is dark and deeply ridged. The small branches are rough and usually covered with fine hairs. Bark on the main stems is dark and deeply plated, lacking the vertical orientation of the furrowed bark of many elms.

Siberian Elm—*Ulmus pumila*

The Siberian elm ranges from 40–60 feet in height. The form may be vase-shaped or an upright oval. The bark of the trunk is rough and ridged. The branches are fine, brittle, and easily broken by strong winds and ice. Litter is a constant battle.

Older twigs are seldom corky. Flowers appear in the spring. This tree is often incorrectly offered in the trade as Chinese elm. The leaves are narrowly rounded to oval in shape. Foliage is 1–3 inches (2½–7½ cm) in length and about half as broad. Leaves are smooth above and glabrous beneath. Foliage is dark green above and smooth and paler green below. Leaf margins have serrate or toothed margins. Petioles are less than ⅛ inch (3 mm) long.

Flower buds are globose and conspicuous during the winter months. Flowers appear early in the spring before leaves and are borne on short stalks. The winged fruit usually appears in early May and is deeply notched at the apex. The seed is off-center, nearly reaching the base of the notch.

The Siberian elm, although storm sensitive, is often planted due to its rapid growth. Siberian elm is tolerant to the Dutch Elm disease (DED) and phloem necrosis (elm yellows) but highly susceptible to the elm-leaf beetle. This tree is often defoliated in early July by the elm-leaf beetle. It has been the major source of resistance to DED in elm breeding programs. Recently it has been replaced in breeding programs by parents that are resistant to the elm leaf beetle as well as DED and elm yellows.

Siberian Elm

Red Mulberry—*Morus rubra*

The red mulberry is native and occurs throughout the state. It prefers the rich soil of the lower and middle districts but is nowhere abundant. It is commonly called mulberry, as there are no other native species. The white mulberry and paper mulberry, which are sometimes found in waste places, are introduced species which have, to some extent, become naturalized. The red mulberry is a small tree, rarely 50 feet high and 2 feet in diameter, often found growing in the shade of larger trees. This tree is quite urban-tolerant.

The leaves are alternate, rounded, or somewhat heart-shaped. Leaves are usually undivided with coarsely toothed margins. Foliage is 3–5 inches (7½–13cm) long, rough, hairy above and soft, hairy beneath. Some of the leaves, especially on young trees and thrifty shoots, are mitten-shaped or variously lobed.

Terminal buds are absent. Buds are imbricate and ⅛–¼ inch (3–6 mm) long. Stems exude milky sap when cut. The bark is rather thin, dark, and grayish-brown and peels off in long, narrow flakes.

May flowers are small and greenish. The flowers are of two kinds on the same or different trees and borne in long, drooping catkins. Female catkins are shorter and appear with the leaves. The fruit is a dark purple aggregate that ripens in July and August and resembles a blackberry. However, a stalk extends through it centrally, and it is longer and narrower than a blackberry. The fruit is sweet and edible and greatly relished by birds and various animals. The fruit can be substituted for blackberries in recipes.

The wood is rather light, soft, not strong, light orange-yellow, and very durable in contact with the soil. It is chiefly used for fence posts. The tree might be planted for this purpose and to furnish food for birds or people. A few selections have been made for fruit quality.

110   114

Red Mulberry

Maclura — Osage-Orange

Osage-oranges are deciduous trees with axillary thorns. Buds are imbricate with few scales. Leaves are alternate, oblong in outline, and have an entire leaf margin. Flowers are dioecious. Fruit is a large, fleshy aggregate structure.

Key to *Maclura* Species

I Stems are thorny, or spiny, and heavily armed. Bark is light green to light brown on medium-sized branches. Trunks are deeply furrowed and dark orange. Sap of fresh twigs is milky. Leaves are 2–5 inches (5–13 cm) long. Flowers bloom in May and June but are not showy. Fruit is green but orange-like in shape and size. The fruit ripens in September.

Maclura (Toxylon) pomifera—Osage-Orange

Description of Species
Osage orange (Bois D'Arc)—
Maclura (Toxylon) pomifera

The osage-orange is found distributed throughout the state, but does not as a rule occur as a forest tree. It grows chiefly in open fields and along fence rows. It was widely planted as a hedge during the last century, as it could retain animals such as bulls and boars. Occasionally it reaches a height of 60 feet and a diameter of 30 inches, but usually it is found from 20–40 feet in height and from 4–12 inches in diameter. This tree is sometimes used for shade or for hedges, but is primarily used as living fence posts.

Osage-Orange (Bois D'Arc)

The leaves are simple, alternate, and oval in outline. The leaf tip is pointed. Foliage is a handsome and lustrous green on the upper surface. Leaves are 2–5 inches (5–12 cm) long and 2–3 inches (5–7½ cm) wide. Foliage color is bright yellow in the autumn.

Terminal buds are absent. Buds are small and partially imbedded in the twig. Stems are thorny, or spiny, and heavily armed. Sap of fresh twigs is milky. Bark is light green to light brown on medium-sized branches and sometimes tinged with yellow. Trunks on old trees are deeply furrowed and have dark orange furrows. The bark contains tannin and has been used for tanning leather.

The yellowish flowers appear in May. They are dioecious. The male flowers are borne in a linear cluster or catkin. Since the male flowers are borne on separate trees, it is possible to select for fruitless trees. Female flowers are round balls that are 1 inch (25 mm) in diameter. The female flower yields the globular, 2–5 inches (5–13 cm) in diameter, fruit that resembles a very rough, green orange, which gives rise to the common name. A selection known as White Sword is thornless and fruitless. White Sword should make an outstanding urban tree.

The wood is heavy, exceedingly hard, very strong, and is durable in contact with the soil. The heartwood is bright orange in color, turning brown upon exposure. It is used largely for posts, sometimes for lumber, and fuel. Because of its strength, the Indians prized the wood for bows and war clubs.

115

Magnolia — Magnolia

Magnolias are deciduous or evergreen trees and shrubs. Buds are valvate with two overlapping scales. The terminal bud is much larger than the lateral buds. Leaves are alternate with entire leaf margins. Stipular scars encircle the twig. Flowers are usually perfect, terminal, large, and showy. Fruit consists of numerous carpels developing into a cone-like structure.

Several magnolias are planted on lawns and in parks for their attractive flowers and foliage. The one most commonly planted is *Magnolia* ×*soulangeana*, which has attractive purplish-pink flowers early in spring before the leaves develop. This tree is not covered since it is a horticultural hybrid that does not escape into the wild.

Key To *Magnolia* Species

I. Leaves are wedge-shaped or rounded at the base.

    A. Leaves are 4–9½ inches (10–24 cm) long. Foliage is dark green above and soft, hairy, and light green beneath. The leaf base is rounded. Twigs are reddish-brown and glossy. Flowers are greenish-yellow and 2¼–3¼ inches (5¾–8½ cm) high. May flowers are followed by a brown, cone-like fruit with red seeds in September or October.

Magnolia acuminata—Cucumbertree Magnolia

    AA. Leaves are 10–24 inches (25–61 cm) long, medium green above, and pale green and hairy beneath with a wedge-shaped leaf base. Twigs and buds are glabrous. Flowers are white with an unpleasant odor. The large flowers are 7¼–10 inches (18½–25 cm) across, and borne above the foliage in May or June. Fruit has a rosy cast to the cone. Seeds are red and ripen in September or October. Tree is often multi-stemmed.

Magnolia tripetala—Umbrella Magnolia

II. Leaves are heart-shaped, or auriculate, with ear-shaped lobes at the base. The huge leaves are 12–32 inches (30½–81 cm) long. Foliage is bloomy and finely hairy beneath. Flowers are creamy white, fragrant, and 10–12 inches (25–30½ cm) across. May and June flowers are followed by rosy fruit in September or October.

Magnolia macrophylla—Bigleaf Magnolia

Description of Species
Cucumbertree Magnolia—
Magnolia acuminata

The cucumbertree attains an average height of 60–80 feet and a diameter of 2–4 feet. It occurs singly or in groups in the eastern half of the state, principally in the northeastern section. Moving southward toward the Ohio River it becomes rare, as it was almost completely removed from the original forests by lumbering. Named selections are available in the nursery trade. 'Miss Honeybee' is smaller in statue and has yellow flowers.

Greenish to white in color, the leaves are pubescent and covered by a single-keeled scale that leaves a distinct scar encircling the twig. The terminal bud may be an inch long, but the lateral buds are half the terminal bud's size. Twigs are reddish-brown and glossy. This is the only one of our native magnolias that has rough bark and a small leaf. The bark is aromatic and bitter to taste. The young twigs are a lustrous reddish-brown. The mature bark of the trunk is rather thin, dark brown, furrowed, and broken into thin scales.

Leaves are 4–9½ inches (10–24 cm) long and 2–4 inches (5–10 cm) wide. The leaves are alternate with an oblong outline; a short, pointed apex; and a rounded leaf base. Foliage is silky, or hairy, when unfolding, becoming smooth to slightly silky with age. Leaf margins are entire and often have wavy edges. Foliage is dark green above and lighter beneath.

Flowers are simple, greenish-yellow, large and 2¼–3¼ inches (5¾-8½ cm) high. May flowers are followed by a brown, cone-like fruit with red seeds. This magnolia has smaller flowers than those of the other native magnolias. The upright petals are whitish-green to yellow. The fruit is a smooth, dark red, often crooked "cone" that is 2½–3 inches (6–7½ cm) long and somewhat resembles a small cucumber. The seeds ripen in September or October, are ½ inch (13 mm) long, and are covered with a pulpy, scarlet coat that attracts birds. The true seeds hang by thin cords from the opening "cones."

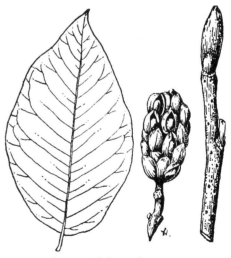

Cucumbertree Magnolia

The wood is light, soft, close-grained, durable, and of a light yellowish-brown color. It is cut and used extensively along with the tulip tree for cabinet making and other similar uses. Besides being a valuable timber tree, it is quite desirable for roadside and ornamental planting.

117

Bigleaf Magnolia—
Magnolia macrophylla

This is a tree similar to the umbrella magnolia but with larger leaves. Some leaves reach a length of nearly 3 feet. Bigleaf magnolia is very rare in Ohio and is reported from one locality in northwestern Jackson County. The tree is sometimes planted for ornamental purposes although it is short-lived, prone to disease, and rather unattractive.

Its huge leaves are 12–32 inches (30½–81 cm) long. Leaf bases are heart-shaped, or auriculate, and have ear-shaped lobes at the base. Foliage color is medium green above and paler beneath. The leaf is bloomy and finely hairy beneath.

Flowers are creamy white, fragrant, and 10–12 inches (25–30½ cm) across. Despite their size, the flowers are usually hidden by the oversized leaves. May and June flowers are followed by rosy fruit in September or October.

The bark is smooth and beech-like. Branches are stout and spreading. The branches form an open, crowned tree in uncrowded conditions. In forest conditions stems are tall and straight.

Bigleaf Magnolia

Umbrella Magnolia—
Magnolia tripetala

Umbrella magnolia is a tree that rarely exceeds 40 feet in height. The tree is made conspicuous by its large leaves and showy, white flowers. This southeastern Ohio native is found in Scioto, Jackson, Vinton, and Hocking counties.

Leaves are 10–24 inches (25–61 cm) long. The foliage is medium green above and pale green and hairy beneath. Umbrella magnolia has a wedge-shaped leaf base. Twigs and buds are glabrous. The trunk and branches are a mottled, light gray color. Widespreading main branches form an open, irregular crown. The tree is often multi-stemmed.

Flowers are white with an unpleasant odor. The large flowers are 7¼–10 inches (18½–25 cm) across but borne above the foliage in May or June. Fruit has a rosy cast to the immature cone. Seeds are red and ripen in September or October.

This species grows in dense thickets along small streams in the rugged hill sections of western Scioto County, now a part of the Shawnee State Forest. Occasionally the umbrella magnolia is planted for ornamental purposes or used as grafting understock for cultivars of other magnolias.

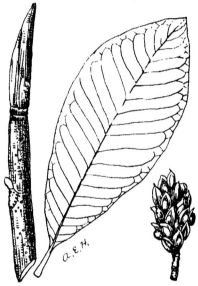

Umbrella Magnolia

Liriodendron — Tuliptree

Tuliptrees are deciduous trees with long, valvate buds. Leaves are lobed and long-petioled. The stipular scar encircles the twig. Flowers are showy, terminal inflorescences. The solitary fruit is a cone-like structure consisting of numerous winged seeds.

Key to *Liriodendron* Species

I. Terminal buds are flattened with two outer scales. Leaf scars are large and nearly round. Leaves are large with three lobes; the terminal one is either square or notched. Flowers are large and greenish-yellow, and they bloom between May and June. Fruit appears in October.

Liriodendron tulipifera—Tulip Tree (Yellow-Poplar)

Description of Species

Tuliptree (Yellow-Poplar)—*Liriodendron tulipifera*

The yellow-poplar received its name from the yellow color of its heartwood. The name "tuliptree" was a result of its attractive, tulip-like flowers. Whatever you wish to call it, tuliptree is one of the largest and more valuable hardwood trees of the United States. It occurs commonly throughout the state except in the central and northwestern sections. The tuliptree reaches its largest size in the deep, moist soils and coves of southeastern Ohio.

Tuliptree (Yellow-Poplar)

The yellow-poplar is most commonly seen at heights of 60–100 feet with diameters of 3–4 feet, although it may attain a much larger size. Young trees have a pyramidal head which in older age becomes more spreading. This tree has a straight, central trunk, like the white pine, and is often clear of limbs for 30–50 feet. The tree has been extensively cut but is reproducing rapidly and remains one of the most abundant and valuable trees in our young, second-growth forests. It is planted for ornamental purposes as well as for shade.

The leaves are simple and 4–6 inches (10–15 cm) in length and breadth. Leaves are distinctive and make this tree easy to identify. The large terminal lobe is either square or notched across the top of the lobe (emarginate). The three-lobed leaves are dark green in the summer and turn a clear yellow in the fall.

Twigs are reddish-brown and glabrous. The stipular scar encircles the twig. Terminal buds are flattened with two outer scales (valvate). The bark of the main trunk is medium gray, and lightly-furrowed vertically, with light gray mottling.

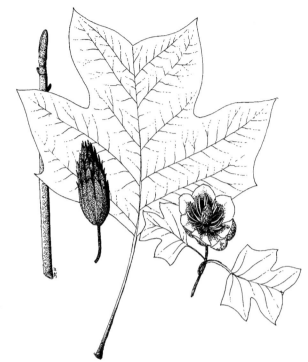

Tuliptree (Yellow-Poplar)

Flowers are borne on branch terminals. The large, greenish-yellow and orange, tulip-shaped flowers appear in May or early June. Flowers are normally hidden from view as they are borne after the foliage is expanded and high in the canopy. Fruit matures in October. The fruit is a narrow, light brown, upright cone 2–3 inches (5–7½ cm) long made up of numerous seeds. Each seed is enclosed in a hard, bony coat with a wing. The winged seed is easily carried by the wind.

The wood is light, soft, and easily worked. Wood is light yellow or brown with a thick, cream-colored sapwood. It is extensively cut into lumber for interior and exterior trim, veneers, turnery, and other high-grade uses.

Asimina — Pawpaw

Pawpaws are deciduous shrubs or small trees with brown, woolly buds bearing two to three outer scales. Leaves are alternate, entire, and large. Flowers are perfect, and the fruit is an edible berry.

Key to *Asimina* Species

I.   This is a small tree, growing 30–35 feet high. Leaves are 6–12 inches (15–30½ cm) long. Flowers are purplish-brown and borne in April or May. Fruit is brownish and ripens in September or October.

Asimina triloba—Common Pawpaw

Description of Species

Common Pawpaw—*Asimina triloba*

The pawpaw is found from western New York and New Jersey, south to Florida, and west to Michigan and Texas. This tree occurs locally in northern Ohio and becomes common in the southern part of the state where it forms thickets on waste areas.

The pawpaw is a dainty tree, rarely exceeding 30 feet in height. This is a forest understory tree.

The leaves are simple, alternate, and 6–12 inches (15–30 cm) long. Foliage is lanceolate in shape with a short, pointed apex and a long, tapering leaf base. The leaf margin is entire. Foliage is medium green and glabrous when mature.

Terminal buds are brown, naked, and flattened. Pawpaw has brown, woolly, lateral buds bearing two to three outer scales. Flower buds are round, ⅙ inch (4 mm) in diameter, very hairy, and dark brown. The twigs are rather slender, smooth, and olive brown with enlarged nodes. The bark is thin, smooth, dark brown, and often dotted with light blotches.

The solitary flowers are large, 1–1½ inches (25–38 mm) wide. Flowers are green at first, turning purplish-brown later, and opening in April or May. Flowers are carried below and hidden by the foliage on short stalks. The fruit suggests a stubby banana. It is 3–5 inches (7½–13 mm) long, green at first, turning yellow, then dark brown when ripe. The fruit contains many dark brown, shiny, flat seeds throughout the flesh. Fruit ripens in September or October but should not be eaten until after being exposed to frost. It is edible, and some say that it tastes like a banana.

Common Pawpaw

This tree is uncommonly planted but has been quite urban-tolerant where it has been used. In open landscapes, this plant has a regular outline and is quite attractive. The wood is soft, weak, yellow to brown in color, and not used commercially.

Sassafras — Sassafras

Sassafras is a deciduous tree with imbricate buds composed of a few scales. Leaves are alternate and have lobed, mitten-shaped, or entire margins. Flowers are polygamous, or dioecious, in several-flowered racemes. Fruit is a drupe.

Key to *Sassafras* Species

I. Branches and foliage are fragrant when crushed. Branching is sympodial. Twigs are glabrous and uniformly green for 1–3 years. The leaves are large, 3¼–4¾ inches (8½–12 cm). Leaves are three-lobed, mitten-shaped, or entire. Flowers are yellow and borne between April and May. Fruit is bluish-black with a red stalk and ripens in September.

Sassafras albidum (variifolium, officinale)—Silky Sassafras

Description of Species
Silky Sassafras—*Sassafras albidum (variifolium, officinale)*

The sassafras is a small, aromatic tree usually not over 40 feet in height or a foot in diameter. It is common throughout the state on dry soils but rarer in the northern half. Sassafras is one of the first broad-leafed trees to come up in abandoned fields where seeds are dropped by birds. The tree also spreads rapidly by root suckers. It is closely related to the camphor tree of Japan.

The leaves are very characteristic. It is one of the few trees with leaves of widely different shapes on the same tree or even on the same twig. The leaves are large, 3¼–4¾ inches (8½–12 cm) long, with entire margins. Some leaves are oval and entire. Others have one lobe resembling the thumb on a mitten, while still others are divided at the outer end into three distinct lobes.

Twigs are glabrous, uniformly green for 1–3 years, and very aromatic. The young leaves and twigs are quite mucilaginous. Branching is sympodial. The bark of the mature trunk is thick, red-brown, and deeply furrowed.

Flowers are yellow and borne in April or May. Fruit is bluish-black with a red stalk and ripens in September.

The flowers are clustered and greenish-yellow. They open with the first unfolding of the leaves. The male and female flowers are usually on different trees (dioecious), but some trees also have perfect flowers with unisexual ones. The fruit is an oblong, dark blue or black, lustrous berry. The berry contains one seed and is surrounded at the base by what appears to be a small, orange-red to scarlet cup at the end of a scarlet stalk.

The wood is light, soft, weak, and brittle. The heartwood is dull orange-brown. At one time it was used for ox yokes. The bark of the roots yields the very aromatic oil of sassafras. This oil is used for flavoring candies and sassafras tea.

Silky Sassafras

123

Liquidambar — Sweetgum

Sweetgums are large, deciduous trees with imbricate buds. Leaves are alternate, palmately lobed, and star-shaped. Flowers are usually monoecious. Fruit is a 1-inch-diameter (2½ cm) head of capsules containing one to two winged seeds in each capsule.

Key to *Liquidambar* Species

I. Leaves are palmately veined with big, star-shaped leaves. Buds and 1-year-old twigs are a glossy brown to greenish. Buds are darker than the twigs. Flowers are yellow and borne in May. Fruit is a brown, 1-inch (2½ cm) ball that matures in November.

Liquidambar styraciflua—American Sweetgum

Description of Species
American Sweetgum—*Liquidambar styraciflua*

The sweetgum, also called redgum and liquidambar, is a handsome tree and native locally in southern Ohio. The sweetgum grows naturally from Connecticut to the southern United States. Another population occurs in Guatemala. In the swamps of the coastal plains it reaches heights of 120 feet and a diameter of 4 feet. In Ohio it occurs locally in Gallia, Lawrence, Scioto, Adams, Brown, and Green counties.

The leaves are simple, alternate, and 3–5 inches (7½–13 cm) long. Leaves are palmately veined with big, star-shaped leaves that are glossy, dark green, and quite handsome. The star-shaped foliage has five points and when crushed, gives off a fragrant odor. In autumn, the leaves turn yellow, pale

American Sweetgum

orange, or deep red. Fall color is outstanding.

The flowers are yellow to green and have two kinds on the same plant. The pollen-bearing flowers are arranged in catkin-like tassels, 2–3 inches (5–7½ cm) long at the top of the inflorescence. The seed-producing flowers occur in long, stalked heads at the base of the inflorescence. The fruit is a long-stalked, 1-inch diameter, round head made up of many capsules, each containing one or two small, winged seeds. The fruit matures in November and can be a serious litter problem.

Buds and 1-year-old twigs are glossy brown to greenish. Buds are darker than the twigs, sharp, pointed, lustrous brown, and fragrant when crushed. The twigs are stout, angular, smooth, and glabrous. Twigs often have corky, winged projections. On younger trunks, bark is smoother and dark gray. The bark on older trunks is deeply furrowed, grayish-brown, and scaly.

The sweetgum is extensively planted as an ornamental tree. This tree has a symmetrical form, grows rapidly, produces unique leaves, and has few serious problems if locally adapted seed sources are used. 'Moraine' and 'Variegata' are cold-hardy selections while some of the California selections ('Festival', 'Palo Alto,' and 'Burgundy') are seriously damaged by temperatures below –10°F. Rotundiloba is reported to be fruitless, but its hardiness is not known. The wood is rather hard, strong, and reddish-brown with white sapwood. It is used for boxes, crates, furniture, and interior finishing.

Platanus — Planetree

Planetrees are large, deciduous trees with buds covered by a single, closed scale. Axillary buds are hidden by the petiole base of a leaf. Terminal buds are absent. Leaves are alternate and lobed. Stipular scars leave a line around the stem when they are shed. Flowers are monoecious. Fruits are an aggregate structure comprised of hard-packed down and seeds. Down expands to assist in seed dispersal in the following spring.

Key to *Platanus* Species

I. There is usually one fruit head in a cluster, but there can be as many as two or three. Leaves have a middle lobe about as long as it is broad. Foliage has three to five lobes and is sparingly toothed. Leaves often have entire margins with the sinuses extending about one-third the length of the blade. Leaf base is truncate. This tree is a hybrid of *P. occidentalis* and *P. orientalis* and flowers in May. Fruit ripens in September to October, but the seeds are shed the following spring. Exfoliating bark is mottled brown, sand, and greenish in color.

Platanus ✕acerifolia—London Planetree

II. Has one, rarely two, fruit heads on a 3-inch (7cm) long pedicel. Lobes are broader than long. Exfoliating bark is creamy white and quite showy. Leaves are three-lobed, occasionally five-lobed with shallow sinuses. Leaf margins are coarsely toothed, or rarely entire. The leaf base is truncate to cordate. This tree is perhaps the largest deciduous tree in North America. Flowers are borne in May and fruit ripens in September or October.

Platanus occidentalis—American Planetree (Sycamore)

Description of Species
London Planetree—*Platanus ✕acerifolia*

A large tree maturing at 100 feet in height, the London planetree is reportedly smaller in dimensions than the American sycamore. This tree is an interspecific hybrid between the American sycamore and oriental planetrees. The London planetree is used extensively for ornamental, street, and park plantings. It has not been as useful in stressful urban sites as was originally suggested. London planetree is marginally cold-hardy in Ohio and is longer-lived when it is grown further south.

The trunk of the tree is straight, tall, and upright; the trunk carries a broad crown. Bark peels off in long strips or flakes, exposing light green or cream-colored new bark. Bark is blotched, or mottled, with sand, gray-brown, and green patches of older bark. The darker bark colors easily distinguish this tree from the American sycamore with its lighter-colored bark.

London Planetree

125

London Planetree

It usually has one, but there may be two to three, fruit heads in a cluster. The tree flowers in May. Fruit ripens in September to October, but the seeds are shed the following spring. The tree is attractive and conspicuous in winter with its mottled bark on the trunk and its button ball fruit hanging from the branches.

Leaves are 4–8 inches (10–20 cm) long with the middle lobe about as long as it is broad. Foliage has three to five lobes and is sparingly toothed. Leaves often have entire margins with the sinuses extending about one-third the length of the blade. The leaf base of the planetree is truncate, while the leaf base of the sycamore is normally cordate or auriculate.

The London planetree has a varied resistance to sycamore anthracnose and is generally more resistant to anthracnose than the American sycamore. The tree is often correctly labeled as disease resistant to this cosmetic disease. However, London planetree is more sensitive to cankerstain than the American sycamore. Cankerstain is normally fatal and is the disease which normally determines the life expectancy of the London planetree. London planetree is shorter-lived than American sycamore. Disease-tolerance does not mean that the tree is tolerant to all diseases.

American Planetree (Sycamore)—*Platanus occidentalis*

This tree, also called sycamore and buttonwood, is perhaps the largest hardwood tree in North America. It occurs throughout Ohio, reaching its larger sizes along streams and on rich bottom lands. Live streams are generally lined with sycamore in Ohio. It is a rapid-growing tree. At maturity it occasionally attains a height of 140–170 feet and a trunk diameter of 10–11 feet. The state champion is 129 feet tall, and 8 feet across with a 15-foot diameter trunk. This tree is the

largest deciduous tree in the United States. The dimensions of this tree are given in Table 1 on page 5. Sycamores often fork into several large, secondary trunks, and the massive, spreading limbs form an open head sometimes 100 feet across.

The bark of this species is a characteristic feature. On younger trunks and large limbs it is very

American Planetree

smooth and greenish-gray in color. The outer bark flakes off yearly in large patches and exposes the nearly white younger bark. The bark color of sycamore is much more showy than the London planetree. Near the base of old trees, the bark becomes thick, dark brown, and divided by furrows.

Twigs are glaucous and yellow-green to brown. Sycamore buds are covered by a single, closed scale. Axillary buds are hidden by the petiole base of a leaf. Terminal buds are absent. Stipular scars leave a line around the stem.

The leaves are simple, alternate, 4–7 inches (10–18 cm) long, and about as broad as they are long. Leaves are three-lobed, occasionally five-lobed, with shallow sinuses. The lobes are broader than long. Leaf margins are coarsely toothed or rarely entire. Foliage is light green and smooth above and paler below. The leaf base is cordate to auriculate and aids in separating this tree from the London planetree. The base of the leaf stalk is hollow, and in falling, exposes the winter bud.

Flowers are green and borne in May, and fruit ripens in September or October. The fruit is a ball about 1 inch (25 mm) in diameter and conspicuous throughout the winter as it hangs on its flexible stem which is 3–5 inches (7½–13 cm) long. The fruit is a good identification feature as sycamore rarely has more than a single fruit per stem, while London planetree usually has several fruits per tree with two or three fruits per pedicel. During early spring, the fruit ball breaks up and the small seeds are widely scattered by wind and water.

The wood is hard and moderately strong, but decays rapidly in contact with the ground. It is used for butchers' blocks, tobacco boxes, furniture, and interior finish.

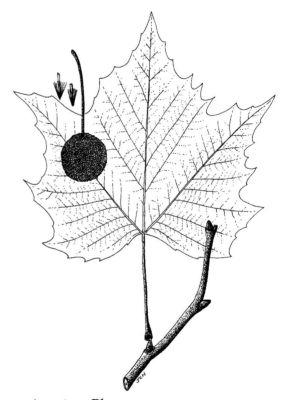

American Planetree

127

Crataegus — Hawthorn

Hawthorns are small, deciduous trees. Most hawthorns are armed. Leaves are alternately arranged with toothed or lobed margins. Flowers are perfect and often showy. Fruit is a pome. These trees are difficult to identify at any time, but especially so in the winter. Those listed here are but a few of the more common hawthorns found in Ohio.

Key to *Crataegus* Species

I. Petioles are 1 inch (2½ cm) long or longer and usually slender.

A. Leaves are medium green, 2–4 inches (5–10 cm) long, and densely pubescent beneath. Leaf margins are sharply double-toothed and often slightly lobed. Flowers are white and bloom in April. Scarlet fruit ripens in August or September.

Crataegus mollis—Downy Hawthorn

AA. Leaves are glabrous or nearly so beneath.

I. Glossy leaves are toothed and without short lobes. Leaves are 2–3¼ inches (5–8½ cm) long, broad, elliptic to obovate in shape with acute to short aciminate leaf tips. Leaf margins are coarsely and doubly serrate. Flowers open in May, followed by red fruit that ripens in October or November.

Crataegus succulenta—Fleshy Hawthorn

II. Leaves have four to five pairs of short, acute lobes. Lobes are usually doubly toothed.

a. Thorns are stout and straight. Leaves are 1¼–2 inches (3–5 cm) long and elliptic or ovate in shape. Leaves are red when unfolding, then become bluish-green. Flowers are white and are borne in May. Fruit is dark purple when it ripens in October.

Crataegus pruinosa—Frosted Hawthorn

aa. Thorns are long and curved. Leaves are ¾–2¼ inches (2–5¾ cm) long and elliptic ovate in shape. Leaf tips are acute. Leaves have three to four pairs of short lobes with doubly toothed margins. Flowers are white and borne in May. Fruit is reddish-brown and ripens in October.

Crataegus intricata—Thicket Hawthorn

II. Petioles are usually short.
A. Leaves are obovate to oblong obovate in shape, usually somewhat clustered, and borne erect above the twigs. Foliage is ¾–3¼ inches (2–8½ cm) long and shiny green and leathery. Thorns are numerous, slender, falcate, and borne on rigid twigs. Flowers are white and borne in May to June. Fruit is dull red and ripens in October and November.

Crataegus crus-galli—Cockspur Hawthorn

AA. Leaves are 2–4 inches (5–10 cm) long with an obovate outline. Leaf margins are irregularly toothed. Leaves on vigorous shoots are slightly lobed above the middle and dull green in color. Thorns are short and stout. Flowers are white and borne in May to June. Fruit is dull red, dotted, and ripens in October.

Crataegus punctata—Dotted Hawthorn

Description of Species
Cockspur Hawthorn—
Crataegus crus-galli

One of the most common of the *Crataegus* is the cockspur hawthorn. Usually a small tree or large shrub, cockspur hawthorn is often foliaged to the ground. Branches are widespreading and borne horizontally. This tree is commonly used for screening where the thorns are not a liability. The foliage is glossy through the growing season. The tree is as wide as it is tall.

Leaves are short-petioled, not lobed, and obovate, or spatulate, in outline. Foliage is deep, glossy green and ¾–3¼ inches (2–8½ cm) long. Leaf tips are usually rounded with finely toothed margins. Leaves are usually somewhat clustered at the end of the twigs and borne erect. The leathery foliage is among the most attractive of all hawthorns. Fall color can be gold to scarlet, but is often not showy.

Thorns are large (up to 2 inches [5 cm]), stiff, and quite sharp. Thorns are numerous, falcate, and borne on rigid twigs. The points of the thorns point downward. Twigs are reddish-brown when young, becoming gray with age.

Flowers are white and borne in May to June. Fruit is a dull red with thin, dry flesh. Fruit is large (½ inch [13 mm] diameter) and falls in October or November. The dense branching attracts nesting birds all year and provides shelter, nesting, and food.

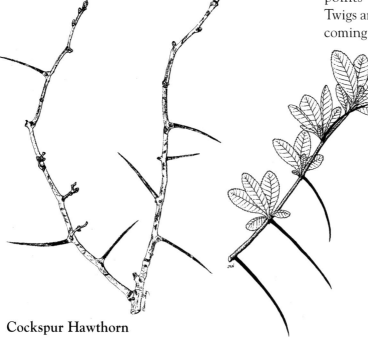

Cockspur Hawthorn

130

Thicket Hawthorn—*Crataegus intricata*

Thicket hawthorn is a small tree or shrub rarely over 10 feet in height. This, too, is a pioneer species and found in fence rows and abandoned fields. The tree is open and unattractive with irregular and spreading branches. Thorns are long and rather stout with curved tips.

Leaves are ¾–2¼ inches (2–5¾ cm) long and elliptic-ovate in shape. Leaves have three to four pairs of short lobes with doubly serrate, or toothed, margins. The upper surface of the leaves is smooth, glossy, and a bright green color. The underside is pale green and nearly smooth. Leaf tips are acute.

Flowers are white and borne in May. Fruit is russet or reddish-brown to yellowish-green in color and of value as food for birds. Fruit ripens in October.

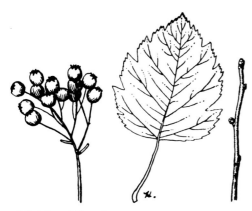

Thicket Hawthorn

Downy Hawthorn—*Crataegus mollis*

Downy hawthorn is a small tree growing to a height of 15–20 feet with stout, spreading branches. Distribution is general over the state. Hawthorns are pioneer invaders and do not persist in the woodlands, as they are killed by the shade of larger, climax forest trees.

The leaves are broad, elliptic to obovate in outline with acute or short, acuminate tips. Leaves are medium green when mature and lighter-colored beneath. Foliage is 2–4 inches (5–10 cm) long and densely pubescent beneath. Later in the season, the hairs are confined to the veins of the leaf. Leaf margins are sharply double-toothed and often slightly lobed. Leaves have four to five pairs of short, acute lobes. Petioles are 1–2 inches (2½–5 cm) long and usually slender.

The spines are stout and 1–1½ inches (25-38 mm) long. Flowers are white and bloom in April or May. The fruit is scarlet, ½ inch (13 mm) across, and pear-shaped. The pome matures in August or September and has a mealy, sweet pulp.

Frosted Hawthorn—*Crataegus pruinosa*

Frosted hawthorn is a small tree reaching heights of 10–20 feet. The branches are widespreading with numerous large, stout, and straight to slightly curved thorns. Frosted hawthorns are pioneer invaders and do not persist in the woodlands but are common in abandoned fields and fence rows, as are other hawthorns.

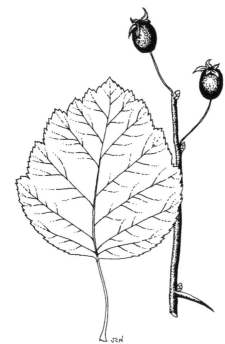

Downy Hawthorn

The leaves are 1¼–2 inches (3–5 cm) long, elliptic or ovate in outline, and taper to an acute leaf tip. Leaves generally have wedge-shaped bases. They have irregularly doubly toothed margins with four to five pairs of short, acute lobes. Leaves are red when unfolding and later become bluish-green above and paler and smooth beneath.

The white flowers are 1 inch (25 mm) across with pink stamens and anthers, giving the flowers a pinkish color. Flowers are borne in May. The fruit is apple green and smooth when nearly ripe, finally turning dark purple when fully ripe. A waxy bloom covers the fruit (pruinose) and gives the tree its scientific and common names. The yellow flesh is sweet when it matures in October.

Dotted Hawthorn—*Crataegus punctata*

A tree or large shrub growing 25–30 feet in height, the dotted hawthorn is found in open, abandoned pastures or in heavily grazed woodland areas. Branches are horizontal or spreading, and

Dotted Hawthorn

133

form a flat-topped tree. Thorns or spines are short and stout. The tree is not as heavily armed as most hawthorns. A thornless cultivar is available in the nursery trade and sold as 'Ohio Pioneer.'

Leaves are 2–4 inches (5–10 cm) long and spatulate in outline. Young foliage is villous above and along veins beneath. Leaf margins are irregularly toothed. Leaves on vigorous shoots are slightly lobed above the middle and dull green in color. Twigs are grayish in color.

Flowers are white and borne in May or early June, after the foliage is expanded. Stamens are often pink. Fruit is deep yellow to dull red and conspicuously dotted. The fleshy fruit is somewhat edible, but drops soon after ripening in October. The fruit falls early enough to attract bees and yellow jackets in large numbers.

Fleshy Hawthorn—*Crataegus succulenta*

Fleshy hawthorn is a small tree growing to 15–20 feet tall. Hawthorns are pioneer invaders and do not persist in the woodlands. They are common in abandoned fields and fence rows. This tree is generally distributed over the state.

Leaves are glossy above but glabrous, or nearly so, beneath. Foliage is 2–3¼ inches (5–8½ cm) long with doubly serrate margins without short lobes. The shape of the leaf is broad, elliptic to obovate, with acute or short, acuminate leaf tips. Leaves have hairs along the veins beneath the leaf.

Flowers are white and borne in May. The bright red fruit ripens in October or November. Fruit is ½ inch (13 mm) across and pulpy. The tree is too small to contain valuable wood.

Sorbus — Mountain-Ash

European mountain-ash has escaped cultivation in northern Ohio but does not threaten native plant populations. These small, deciduous trees have rather large, scaly buds. Pinnately compound leaves are borne alternately along the stems. Flowers are showy, perfect, and borne in flat-topped corymbs. Fruit is a red pome and borne in showy clusters.

Key to *Sorbus* Species

      I. Winter bud scales are white, woolly, and not sticky. Young branches are pubescent. Leaves are odd-pinnate with nine to 15 leaflets that are ¾–2 inches (2–5 cm) long. Stipules are broad and coarsely toothed. Flowers are white and borne in May. Fruit is orange-red and matures in August or September.

Sorbus aucuparia—European Mountain-Ash

      II. Winter bud scales are glabrous, or ciliate at the most, and sticky. Young branches rapidly become glabrous. Leaves are odd-pinnate with 11–17 leaflets that are 1½–4 inches (4–10 cm) long. Flowers are white and borne in May. Fruit is bright red and matures in October.

Sorbus americana—American Mountain-Ash

Description of Species

American Mountain-Ash—*Sorbus americana*

American mountain-ash is a small tree, sometimes appearing as a shrub, that reaches 10–20 feet in height with attractive foliage and fruit. This tree is native in areas of Ohio with cooler summers. It occurs from Nova Scotia, Canada, south along the Appalachian Mountain spine to North Carolina. American mountain-ash is found in cool, mountain valleys. This tree should be grown only in the lake-effect areas of Ohio.

Winter buds scales are glabrous, or ciliate at the most, and sticky. Young branches rapidly become glabrous. These characteristics readily separate this tree from the European mountain-ash. Leaves are odd-pinnate with 11–17 leaflets that are 1½–4 inches (4–10 cm) long and of a light green color.

White flowers are smaller than the European mountain-ash and borne in May. Cymes are 2½–5 inches (6–13 cm) across. The individual flower is only ¼ inch (6 mm) across. Fruit is bright red and matures in October.

European Mountain-Ash (Rowan Tree)—*Sorbus aucuparia*

The European mountain-ash is an attractive tree planted for ornamental purposes and grown for the showy, orange-red fruit. It is a round-headed tree that grows to 50 feet. Numerous cultivars are available in the nursery trade. This tree grows well only in the lake-effect areas of Ohio. This tree generally performs poorly and is short-lived in Ohio landscapes away from Lake Erie.

Winter bud scales are large, white, woolly, and not sticky. Young branches are pubescent. Leaves are odd-pinnate with nine to 15 leaflets. Leaflets are smaller than the American mountain-ash leaflets at ¾–2 inches (2–5 cm) long. Stipules are broad and coarsely toothed.

135

The tree is usually many-branched with smooth, grayish bark. Flowers are white, ⅓ inch (8 mm) in diameter. Flowers are larger than the American counterpart and borne in May in cymes that are 4–6 inches (10-15 cm) across. Fruit is orange-red and matures in August or September. Fruit forms a massive, 4–6-inch (10–15 cm) head of orange-red pomes in fall. Fruit is favored as food for birds and normally is retained until the end of the year.

European Mountain-Ash

Malus — Crabapple

Crabapples are deciduous, small trees or shrubs with imbricate (scaly) buds. Leaves are toothed or lobed. Flowers are perfect and showy. Fruit is the classic example of a pome and is usually conspicuous. Many species and cultivars are planted as small, ornamental trees with attractive flowers and fruits. The native species is given below.

Key to *Malus* Species

I. Leaves are ovate to oblong and 2–4 inches (5–10 cm) long. Leaf margins are irregularly toothed or sparingly lobed on young shoots. Small, short, threadlike, black glands are present on the upper midrib of the leaves. Flowers are pink, fading to white. Flowers pleasantly scent the May landscape. Fruit is greenish and ripens in September.

Malus coronaria—Wild Sweet Crabapple

Description of Species
Wild Sweet Crabapple—*Malus coronaria*

Sweet crab is a spreading tree of small to medium size reaching 10–30 feet in height. The tree is urban-tolerant but must be used where the falling fruit does not cause trouble and where the defoliation by apple scab is not a concern.

Leaves are ovate to oblong and 2–4 inches (5–10 cm) long. Leaf margins are irregularly toothed. Vigorous shoots are sparingly lobed. The medium green leaves have acute leaf tips and usually have rounded leaf bases. New leaves are hairy, becoming smooth (glabrous). Small, short, threadlike, black glands are present on the upper midrib of the leaves.

Buds are reddish-brown and ovoid in shape. Twigs are lightly armed. Some twigs are modified as spines. Spines are more commonly found in the interior of the tree.

The flowers are pink, sometimes fading to white, and very fragrant. The attractive flowers resemble the common apple bloom. Flowers scent the May landscape. Fruit is greenish and ripens in September. The fruit is large (1 inch [25 mm] diameter) and can create a litter problem as the deteriorating fruit attracts bees and wasps. Fruit can be used to make crabapple jelly.

136

Amelanchier — Serviceberry, Shadbush, Juneberry

Serviceberries are small, deciduous trees or shrubs with conspicuous terminal buds. Buds are long and pointed with several (four to five) scales. Leaves are alternate, toothed, and have nearly straight veins. Flowers are perfect and showy. Fruit is a berrylike pome. The species of serviceberries are exceedingly difficult to identify. There are a number of species in Ohio but only the common downy serviceberry will be discussed here. The nursery trade offers many named cultivars that are *Amelanchier* ×*grandiflora*, or apple serviceberry, selections. Apple serviceberry is a naturally occurring hybrid between *Amelanchier arborea* and *Amelanchier laevis* (Allegheny serviceberry). *Amelanchier canadensis* is multi-stemmed and more shrub-like than the others discussed here.

Key to *Amelanchier* Species

> I. Bark is smooth and gray. Leaves have acute leaf tips with rounded leaf bases and are 1¼–3¼ inches (3–8½ cm) long. Flowers are white and bloom in April or May. Flowers bloom before the leaves have expanded. Fruit is purple and ripens in June.
>
> *Amelanchier arborea*—Downy Serviceberry

Description of Species
Downy Serviceberry— *Amelanchier arborea*

The serviceberry, also known as Juneberry, shadbush, and shadblow, is found throughout Ohio but attains its best development in the hills of the eastern portion of the state. Serviceberry is a small- to medium-sized tree growing 20–50 feet high. The tree has a narrow, rounded top but is often little more than a shrub.

The bark is thin, ashy-gray, and smooth on the branches and upper part of the stem, resulting in a beech-like look to the bark. Older bark

Downy Serviceberry

breaks into shallow fissures on the short trunk. Trees may be single or multi-leadered with main stems ranging from 6–18 inches (15–46 cm) in diameter. Overwintering buds are more than ½ inch (13 mm) long and pointed with several (four to five) scales.

The leaves are alternate, slender-stalked, and have finely toothed leaf margins. Leaves have acute leaf tips with rounded leaf bases and are 1¼–3¼ inches (3–8½ cm) long. Foliage color is a light green. Leaves have nearly straight veins. Early in the season the foliage is covered with scattered, silky hairs. Hairs are more common beneath the leaves.

The white flowers appear in erect or drooping racemes in April or May, either before or with the leaves. The flowers make the tree quite conspicuous in the leafless or budding forest. Flowers are ¾ inch (19 mm) across and quite apple-like, since the serviceberries are closely related to apples.

Fruit is ⅓ inch (8 mm) in diameter and ripens in June. The fruit is sweet and edible, and it can be a substitute for blueberries in most recipes. Birds and other denizens of the forest, including man, are very fond of the fruit and have been known to destroy the trees to gather one good crop of fruit. Today it is rare to find a tree full of fruit. Birds start eating the berries as soon as they begin to ripen and often before they are desirable for human consumption.

The wood is heavy, exceedingly hard, strong, close-grained, and dark brown. It is occasionally used for handles. This is a desirable ornamental tree and should be planted for this purpose and for bird food. In fact, it will be hard to beat the birds to the fruit.

Downy Serviceberry

138

Prunus — Plum, Cherry

Plums and cherries are deciduous or evergreen trees or shrubs with imbricate buds. Evergreen species are not cold-hardy in Ohio and will not be discussed. Twigs have a bitter, almond taste. Leaves are alternate and toothed. Flowers are perfect and often showy. Fruit is a drupe and usually has a single seed.

Key to *Prunus* Species

I. The end bud is a lateral (pseudo-terminal) bud, and terminal buds are absent. A close examination of the twig will show a small branch stub at the end. Leaves are 2½–4 inches (6–10 cm) long. Glands on petioles are often lacking, even on young growth. Twigs are glabrous. Flowers are white, and fruit is red or yellowish.

Prunus americana—American Plum

II. Terminal buds are present.

A. Buds are usually clustered at the ends of twigs in an oak-like fashion. Small, round glands on petioles are often missing, even on young growth. Glabrous leaves are 2½–4½ inches (6–11 cm) long. Petioles are ½–⁴/₅ inches (13–20 mm) long. Twigs are glabrous, slender, reddish, and shiny. Flowers are white and borne solitarily, or few flowers in a cluster. Fruit is a red drupe.

Prunus pensylvanica—Pin Cherry

AA. Buds are usually not clustered at ends of twigs. Terminal buds are larger and more pointed than the lateral buds. Glands on petioles are always present. Leaves are medium green above and light green beneath. Foliage is oblong, widest at or below the middle, and 2–4 inches (5–10 cm) long. Flowers are white and bloom between May and June. Flowers are borne in a many-flowered raceme. Fruit is black and ripens in September or October.

Prunus serotina—Wild Black Cherry

Description of Species

American (Wild) Plum—*Prunus americana*

American plum is a small tree occurring in patches or thickets usually along the borders of woods or in abandoned fields. The trees are shade intolerant. The trees are often dwarf and rarely exceed 15 feet in height. This species reproduces both by seed and root sprouts. The suckering characteristic makes this tree difficult to use in the landscape.

Leaves are 2½–4 inches (6–10 cm) long. Glands on petioles are often lacking, even on young growth. Leaves are rounded at the base and taper gradually to an acute or sharp point. The margins are finely, and often doubly, toothed.

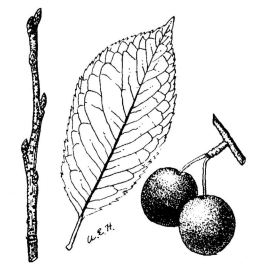

American (Wild) Plum

139

Terminal buds are absent. End buds are pseudo-terminal buds. A close examination of the twig will show a small branch stub at the end where the terminal growth aborted. The glabrous branches are black to reddish-brown in color. Twigs have thornlike spurs.

When in bloom, the trees are a mass of white, highly fragrant flowers. Flowers appear before the leaves in April or May. The fruit is globular or rounded with thick, red to yellow skin that ripens in June or July. Early settlers of Ohio valued wild plums for jelly, plum butter, and preserves.

Pin (Wild Red) Cherry

Pin (Wild Red) Cherry— *Prunus pensylvanica*

Pin cherry is a small tree usually not more than 30 feet in height. Branches are slender, smooth, brown to reddish in color, and glossy. Pin cherry occurs sparsely in northern Ohio, usually following a disturbance such as clear cutting or fire. The tree is not shade-tolerant and does not persist in woodlands.

Terminal buds are present. Twigs are glabrous, slender, reddish, and shiny. Buds are usually clustered at the ends of twigs in an oak-like fashion. Small, round glands on petioles are often missing, even on young growth. Glabrous leaves are 2½–4½ inches (6–11¾ cm) long. Petioles are ½–⅘ inches (13–20 mm) long. Leaves are narrow to oval in shape and gradually taper to an acute tip. Leaf margins are finely and sharply toothed.

Flowers open in May or June and are quite showy and attractive. Flowers are white and borne as solitary flowers or a few in a cluster. Fruit is a ¼ inch-diameter (6 mm), globular, red drupe. The sour fruit ripens in July and August and is attractive to birds. The trees are too small to have valuable timber.

Wild Black Cherry—
Prunus serotina

Wild black cherry is a medium-sized tree up to 70 feet high with a 1–3-foot-diameter trunk. As a tree, the black cherry is at its best in the moist, deep soils of southern Ohio. Forest trees have long, clear trunks with little taper. Open-grown trees have short trunks with many branches and irregular-spreading crowns. Wild cherry is much more shade-tolerant as a young tree than other native cherries and is found in mature woodlands.

Foliage is oblong, widest at or below the middle, and 2–4 inches (5–10 cm) long. The leaves are alternate, simple, and have leaf margins that are broken by many fine, incurved teeth. Leaves are medium green above and light green beneath. Glands on the petioles are always present.

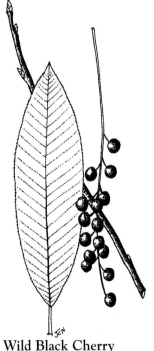

Buds are not clustered at the ends of twigs. Terminal buds are present, larger, and more pointed than the lateral buds. The bark on branches and young trunks is smooth, bright reddish-brown, and glossy. Twigs are marked by conspicuous, narrow, white, horizontal lines (lenticels). The twigs have a bitter, almond taste. On older trunks the bark becomes rough and broken into thick, irregular plates.

Flowers are white and open in May or June. Flowers are borne in a many-flowered raceme. Fruit is a black drupe and ripens in September or October. The fruit is dull, purplish-black, about as large as a pea, and borne in long, hanging clusters. Fruit is edible although it has a slightly bitter taste. The fruit can be fermented to make cherry brandy.

The wood is reddish-brown with yellowish sapwood. Cherry lumber is moderately heavy, hard, strong, and fine-grained. Cherry does not warp or split in seasoning. It is valuable for its luster and color and is used for furniture and interior finish. With the exception of black walnut, cherry lumber has a greater unit value than any other native hardwood of the eastern United States.

141

Wild Black Cherry

Cercis — Redbud

Redbuds are small- to medium-sized deciduous trees. Winter buds have several scales and are superposed. Leaves are alternate, entire, large, and palmately veined. Flowers are usually bisexual and showy. Fruit is a flat pod.

Key to *Cercis* Species

I. The leaves are round or broadly ovate and are palmately veined with cordate leaf bases. Leaves are 2¾–4¾ inches (7–12 cm) long. Rosy pink, pealike flowers bloom in April or May and are followed by brown, pea-pod-like fruit in September or October.

Cercis canadensis—Eastern Redbud

Eastern Redbud

Description of Species
Eastern Redbud—*Cercis Canadensis*

The redbud is sometimes called the Judas tree from its oriental relative of the same name. Redbud is a woodland-edge tree occurring under taller trees, or on the borders of hillside fields and in valleys throughout the state except in the northeastern portion. In western Ohio, redbud is abundant. It ordinarily attains a height of 25–50 feet and a trunk diameter of 6–12 inches. Stout branches usually form a wide, flat head.

The leaves are alternate with entire leaf margins. Leaves are 2¾–4¾ inches (7–12 cm) long. Round or broadly ovate leaves are palmately veined with cordate leaf bases. Foliage is glossy green, turning a bright, clear yellow in autumn.

Eastern Redbud

Winter buds have several scales and are superposed. The bark on young branches is bright reddish-brown, while the mature bark divides into long, narrow plates that separate into thin scales.

The conspicuous, bright pink to purplish-red, pea-shaped flowers are in clusters along the twigs and small branches. The inflorescence is usually bisexual and showy. Flowers appear before, or with, the leaves in April or May. Redbuds often flower at the same time as the native, white-flowered, flowering dogwood.

The fruit is an oblong, flattened pod with many seeds, 2–4 inches (5–10 cm) long. Pods are green at first, then turn red, and then brown when ripe in September or October. The fruit often hangs on the trees most of the winter.

The wood is heavy; hard; not strong; rich, dark brown in color; and of little commercial importance. The redbud is cultivated as an ornamental tree and for that purpose might be planted more generally in Ohio. While named cultivars have been introduced, they are difficult to propagate asexually and are rarely found. The tree is short-lived as an ornamental but reseeds itself readily. This woodland-edge tree does not do well in full sun and seems to require a partially shaded situation.

143

Gleditsia — Honeylocust

Honeylocusts are large, deciduous trees. Native trees usually bear stout, often branched, spines. Winter buds are small and superposed. Leaves are alternate and compound, or twice compound. Leaflets are small. Unisexual and bisexual flowers are found on the same plant. The fruit is a large, compressed pod.

Key to *Gleditsia* Species

I. Buds are very minute and hidden. Thorns are long, stout, and clustered on the trunk and branches. Spines are often branched and may exceed 15 inches (38 cm) in length. Leaves are normally pinnately compound, but may be bipinnately compound on vigorous shoots. Leaflets are only slightly toothed and nearly sessile (not stalked). Flowers are greenish-white and bloom in June. Fruit follows in October and persists into December.

Gleditsia triacanthos—Common Honeylocust

Common Honeylocust

Description of Species
Common Honeylocust—*Gleditsia triacanthos*

The honeylocust tree occurs scattered throughout the state, although it is more common in the southwestern section. It grows under a wide variety of soil and moisture conditions. It sometimes occurs in the forest, but more commonly in corners and waste places beside roads and fields. It grows to a diameter of 30 inches and a height of 75 feet.

The leaves are alternate, odd-pinnate or twice compound, and feather-like with 18–28 leaflets. Pinnate leaves are 6–8 inches (15–20 cm) long and resemble the leaf of the black locust. Twice pinnate leaves consist of four to seven pairs of pinnate, or secondary, leaflets. Leaflets are ¾–1½ inches (19–38 mm) long and medium green in color. Leaflets are only slightly toothed and nearly sessile (not stalked).

Terminal buds are conspicuously absent. Winter buds are very minute, hidden, and superposed. The bark on old trees is dark gray and is divided into thin, tight scales.

This species has strong thorns that are straight, brown, sharp, and shiny. Unbranched spines are found on the 1-year-old twigs and remain for many years. The main stem has thorns that are often branched and as long as 15 inches (38 cm). The thorns along the main stem are spectacular and borne in clusters that sometimes obscure the bark. The thorns are sufficient to identify native honeylocust.

Flowers are greenish-white and bloom in June. A single raceme has many male flowers and a few perfect flowers. Some of the nursery selections have been selected for a tendency to produce reduced numbers of perfect flowers. Sometimes they are listed as fruit-less, but this is not true. They should be listed as showing reduced fruiting. Fruit follows in October and persists well into December. The fruit is a pod, 10–18 inches (25–45 cm) long, often twisted, 1–1½ inches (25–38 mm) wide, flat, dark brown or black when ripe, and containing yellow, sweetish pulp and seeds. The seeds are very hard, and each is separated from the others by the pulp. The pods are eaten by many animals. Since the seeds are hard to digest, many seeds pass through the digestive system and are widely scattered from the parent tree. The wood is coarse-grained, hard, and strong.

Thornless selections of common honeylocust are commonly planted as ornamentals. This tree makes a beautiful lawn tree and is well adapted for street and ornamental planting. Numerous named culti-vars are available for landscape planting and avoid the obvious problems that the thorns represent. Among the Ohio introductions are 'Imperial,' 'Mo-raine,' 'Shademaster,' and 'Skyline.' The variety *inermis* is a naturally occurring seedling that is thorn-less, or nearly so.

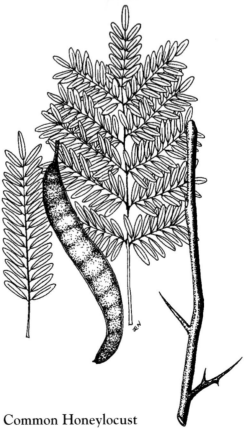

Common Honeylocust

145

Robinia — Locust

Locusts are deciduous trees or shrubs. Winter buds are small and hidden. Terminal buds are absent. Leaves are alternate, compound and odd-pinnate. Branchlets usually have stipular thorns. Pink to white flowers are borne in showy, pendulous racemes. The fruit is a pod.

Key to *Robinia* Species

I. Side buds are usually hidden by the petiole base or sunken beneath the leaf scar. Thorns are 1 inch (2½ cm) long and unbranched. Twigs are glabrous or only slightly hairy. Leaves are normally pinnately compound with seven to 19 leaflets. Leaflets have entire leaf margins. Flowers are white, very fragrant, and bloom in June. Fruit follows in September.

Robinia pseudoacacia—Black (Yellow) Locust

Description of Species
Black (Yellow) Locust—*Robinia pseudoacacia*

The black locust occurs throughout the state in all soils and moisture conditions except swamps. Forest trees of black locust occur in the eastern and southeastern portions of the state. As a forest tree, it attains heights of 80–100 feet and diameters of 30 inches. In other sections of the state it occurs in thickets on clay banks and waste places or singularly in fencerows and is normally smaller in statue.

The leaf is alternate, odd-pinnate, and feather-like with seven to 19 leaflets. Pinnate leaves are feather-like and 6–10 inches (15–25 cm) long. Leaflets are ¾–1½ inches (19–38 mm) long and medium green in color. Leaflets are oblong and have entire leaf margins. Foliage is often brown by mid-summer due to the feeding of the black locust leaf miner.

Terminal buds are conspicuously absent. Side buds are usually hidden by the petiole base or sunken beneath the leaf scar. Twigs are glabrous, or only slightly hairy, and a glossy, dark brown. Twigs and branchlets are armed with straight or slightly curved spines up to 1 inch (25 mm) long. Spines are unbranched and may remain attached to the branch for many years.

June flowers are fragrant and white to ivory in color. Showy flowers are borne in pendant racemes up to 8 inches (20 cm) long. Flowers are the source of nectar for a preferred honey. Flowers are followed in September by a dark brown, pea-like pod from 3–5 inches (8–13 cm) long. The pod splits during the winter scattering some seed while others remain attached to the two halves. The split pods later act as wings to disperse the remaining seeds before the strong spring winds.

The bark is dark brown and divides into strips as the tree ages. Wood is yellow in color, coarse-grained, dense, and heavy. The heartwood is very durable in contact with the soil and is widely used for fence posts. The wood is also used for insulator pins, lumber, and fuel.

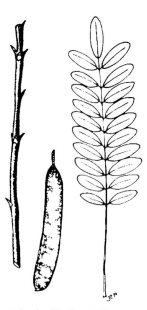

Black (Yellow) Locust

Gymnocladus — Kentucky Coffeetree

Coffeetrees are large, deciduous trees with stout branches. Twigs have large pith chambers and small, reddish, superposed winter buds. Terminal buds are absent. Leaves are twice compound with entire margined leaflets. Flowers are borne in terminal panicles. Fruit is a thick, flat pod.

Key to *Gymnocladus* Species

I. Leaves are composed of three to seven pinnae (leaf divisions), usually with six to 14 leaflets each. Leaves are large, 12–30 inches (30½–76 cm) long with numerous, small, entire leaflets. Fall foliage is yellow. Branches are stout and often glaucous (bloomy).

Gymnocladus dioicus—Kentucky Coffeetree

Winter buds are small, reddish, and often placed above one another in close formation (superposed). Terminal buds are absent. The buds are small, downy, almost entirely imbedded in twigs, and surrounded by a hairy ring of bark. The bark is dark gray to blackish-brown, and roughened by long, shallow furrows. The twigs are very stout, greenish-brown, often covered with a crusty coating marked with large, broad, heart-shaped leaf scars. Twigs contain a wide, pinkish to brown pith.

The flowers appear in June and are of two kinds. Male and female flowers are borne on separate trees. Flowers are greenish-white and grouped in panicles. Female panicles are up to 12 inches (30 cm) long while male flower clusters are denser and only 3–4 inches (7½–10 cm) long. The pods result from the female flowers and contain six to nine marble-like brown seeds. Pods are 6–10 inches (15–25 cm) long and mature in October. The conspicuous pods often persist far into the winter.

The wood is rather heavy, coarse-grained, and light brown to reddish-brown in color. It is used for general construction work. The common name of this tree derives from the one- time use of the roasted seeds as an inferior substitute for coffee.

Description of Species
Kentucky Coffeetree—*Gymnocladus dioicus*

The Kentucky coffeetree is found from central New York to Tennessee and west to Minnesota and Oklahoma. It is common on limestone soils of southern and southwestern Ohio. It is rare north of Franklin County, and is seldom found in the unglaciated section in southeastern Ohio.

One of the most striking characteristics of the tree is its outline during the winter. Standing in the open, the tree appears rugged and coarse in outline. The branches are heavy and thick, apparently with no twigs. Lacking foliage the tree presents a decidedly naked appearance as if heavily pruned.

The leaves are alternate, twice compound, 1–2½ feet (30½–76 cm) long, and 1–2 feet (30–61 cm) wide. The leaflets are egg-shaped and about 2 inches (5 cm) long. The foliage has a sharp, pointed apex and an entire to undulate leaf margin. Leaves are hairy when young, becoming glabrous later. Flowers are borne in terminal panicles. Fruit is a thick, flat pod.

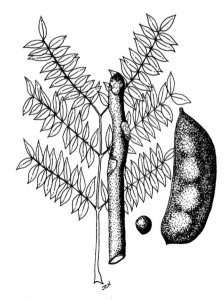

Kentucky Coffeetree

Zanthoxylum — Pricklyash

Pricklyash is a small, deciduous tree or shrub usually with prickles. Branchlets and leaves are aromatic when crushed. Winter buds are small and superposed. Leaves are alternate and odd-pinnate with five to 11 leaflets per leaf. Flowers are dioecious or polygamous and small. Fruit is a dry follicle.

Key to *Zanthoxylum* Species

I. Prickles are found mostly in pairs below the stipules. Leaflets are either slightly toothed or entire. Buds are reddish and woolly. Leaf scars are white. Flowers are small, yellow-green, and flower in April or May. Fruit is black and ripens in August.

Zanthoxylum americanum—Common Pricklyash (Toothache-Tree)

Description of Species
Common Pricklyash (Toothache-Tree)—
Zanthoxylum americanum

A small tree or shrub usually not exceeding 15–20 feet in height, pricklyash is found in thickets and second-growth woodlands in western Ohio. Pricklyash is less common in the eastern portion of the state. This plant is a source of xanthoxylin which is used in some medical preparations and at one time was used as a folk cure for a toothache.

Common Pricklyash (Toothache-Tree)

Leaves are alternate, odd-pinnately compound with five to 11 leaflets per leaf. Leaflets are dark green above and pale green beneath. Leaflets are either slightly toothed or entire and pubescent beneath. Foliage is aromatic.

Winter buds are small and superposed. Buds are reddish and woolly. Leaf scars are white. Young twigs are covered with soft, fine hairs. Branches are covered with prickles that are painful to touch. Prickles are found mostly in pairs below the stipules.

Flowers are small, dioecious or polygamous, and borne in axillary clusters before the foliage emerges. April or May flowers are small and yellow to yellowish-green in color. The aromatic fruit follows on the female plant. Fruit is berrylike with a one- to two-seeded follicle. Fruit is black and ripens in August.

149

Ptelea — Hoptree (Wafer-Ash)

Crushed foliage and branches are pungent in this small, deciduous tree. Buds are superposed and small; terminal buds are absent. Leaves are trifoliate with entire leaf margins. Flowers are small with unisexual and bisexual flowers on the same plant. Fruit is a round samara.

Key to *Ptelea* Species

I. Leaflets are trifoliate. Buds are often hidden by the leaf base and are silvery and silky. Leaf scars are horseshoe-shaped. Branches are reddish-brown in the second year. Flowers are greenish-white, unpleasantly scented, and bloom in June. Fruit matures in September or October.

Ptelea trifoliata—Common Hoptree (Wafer-Ash)

Description of Species

Common Hoptree (Wafer-Ash)—*Ptelea trifoliata*

This is a small tree or a large shrub depending upon where the plant grows. Wafer-ash is found scattered over the state. The bark and leaves are bitter, strongly scented, and posses tonic qualities. It has a straight, slender trunk, 6–8 inches (15–20 cm) diameter, and seldom reaches a height of more than 20 feet.

The leaves are composed of three leaflets (trifoliate), rarely five, with entire leaf margins. Each leaflet is oval or pear-shaped with a pointed tip. Leaflets are 4–6 inches (5–15 cm) long by 2–3 inches (5–7½ cm) wide, and dark green on the upper surface. The central leaflet is the largest.

Terminal buds are absent. Buds are superposed, small, silvery, silky, and often hidden by the leaf base. Leaf scars are horseshoe-shaped. Branches are reddish-brown in the second year.

Flowers are small with unisexual and bisexual flowers on the same plant. Flowers are greenish-white and unpleasantly scented. This tree flowers in June. Fruit matures in September or October. The fruit consists of a small, round, two-seeded, winged samara resembling paper caps for toy pistols. They occur in dense, drooping clusters and hang on the tree over winter. Fruit matures in September or October.

The wood is heavy, hard, yellowish-brown, and close-grained. The trees are too small and widely scattered to be commercially important. The bitter bark of the roots is sometimes used as a tonic.

Ailanthus — Tree of Heaven

Known as the tree of heaven, the *Ailanthus* is an exotic, deciduous tree. Stout twigs have rounded buds bearing two to four scales with an absent terminal bud. The ill-scented leaves are alternate, odd-pinnate, and 12–24 inches (30–60 cm) long. There are 11–25 leaflets which often bear a few teeth near the base with glands beneath. Flowers are small and dioecious. The male flowers are reported to give off an unpleasant odor that may be masked by the odor of the foliage. Fruit is a flattened samara about 1½ inches (4 cm) long.

Key to *Ailanthus* Species

I. All portions of the tree are ill-scented. Leaves are large, 12–24 inches (30½–61 cm) long with 11–25 leaflets. Leaflets are acute-tipped with a few glandular teeth at the base. Plant is a rapidly growing tree. Twigs are stout with brown pith and imbricate buds. Flowers are yellowish and borne in June or July. Fruit is reddish-brown and matures in September or October.

Ailanthus altissima (glandulosa)—Tree of Heaven, Ailanthus

Description of Species

Ailanthus (Tree of Heaven)—*Ailanthus altissima (glandulosa)*

The *Ailanthus* was brought to this country from China about 185 years ago and was first planted near Philadelphia, Penn. The *Ailanthus* has been planted in all parts of Ohio. It has escaped cultivation and may form dense thickets in disturbed sites. It is also called tree of heaven and is common in waste places, roadways, and abandoned fields. All portions of the tree are ill-scented and some suggest that it is called the tree of heaven because it smells all the way to heaven.

The leaves are 12–24 inches (30½–61 cm) long, alternate, odd-pinnately compound, and have 11–25 leaflets per leaf. Leaflets are 3–5 inches (7½–13 cm) long, lanceolate, and long-pointed at the apex. Leaflets are acute-tipped with a few glandular teeth at the base. Glands are usually present near the base of leaflets.

Ailanthus (Tree of Heaven)

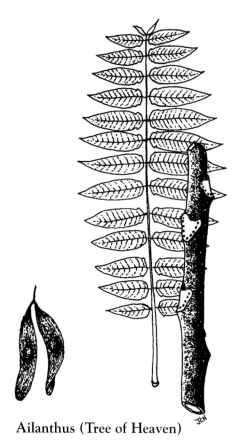

Ailanthus (Tree of Heaven)

Twigs are stout with brown pith and imbricate buds. The terminal bud is absent. The buds are ⅛–⅙ inches (3–4 mm) long, round, and reddish-brown with two visible scales located in a notch above the large leaf scar. The bark on young trees is smooth, thin, and light gray. Bark on older trunks becomes dark gray to black. The twigs are very stout, yellowish-green to brown, and covered with a velvety down. Twigs are marked with ocher-colored breathing pores (lenticels) and large, heart-shaped leaf scars with eight to 14 groups of bundle scars.

The individual flowers are small, dioecious, greenish, and borne in June or July. Flowers are arranged in loose panicles. Pollen-bearing and seed-producing flowers occur on different trees. The male flowers give off an unpleasant odor that may be masked by the odor of the foliage. The fruit is a thin, winged samara about 1½ inches (38 mm) long and produced in large clusters. Seed heads are green at first, then reddish-brown, and then tan. Fruit is held until the winter. Seeds mature in September or October, sometimes with a red, fruited stage between the green and the brown stages.

The wood is light, soft, weak, and white to pale yellow. It is well-adapted to the manufacture of paper pulp. Male trees produce no seed or seedlings and might be preferred for landscape plantings. A male cultivar was recently introduced as 'Metro.'

Rhus — Sumac

Sumacs are deciduous shrubs, small trees, or vines with small, naked buds. Leaves are alternate and odd-pinnate. Flowers are dioecious, or have unisexual and bisexual flowers on the same plant. Fruit is a drupe. Some plants, such as poison ivy, are highly poisonous.

Key to *Rhus* Species

I. Twigs are densely hairy. Flowers are greenish and open in June or July. Fruits are crimson, hairy, and ripen in August.

Thus typhina—Staghorn Sumac

II. Twigs are not hairy or only minutely so.
   A. Buds are minutely hairy. Twigs are stout and vigorous. Rachis (axis bearing leaflets) is not winged. Flowers are greenish and bloom in July or August. Fruit is scarlet and ripens in August or September.

   Rhus glabra—Smooth Sumac

   AA. Buds are not hairy. Twigs are not as stout and vigorous as the smooth sumac. Twigs are often minutely pubescent.
      I. Rachis is winged. Leaflets have a few teeth, or are nearly entire, and glossy green. Flowers are greenish and flower in June or July. Fruits are crimson and ripen in September or October.

      Rhus copallina—Winged Sumac

      II. Leaflet stem (rachis) is not winged. Plant is *poisonous to the touch*, and grows only in bogs or wet soil. There are seven to 13 leaflets per leaf. Flowers are greenish-yellow and bloom in June or July. Fruit is yellow to gray and matures in September.

      Rhus (Toxicodendron) vernix—Poison Sumac

Description of Species
Winged Sumac (Shining Sumac)— *Rhus copallina*

The winged or shining sumac is a nonpoisonous sumac. It is native in the Allegheny Plateau regions of Ohio and is most common in the southeastern part of the state. Winged sumac rarely exceeds 15 feet in height. It furnishes a bright red accent to the landscape during the fall, and is frequently found in large clumps.

The rachis is winged and a good identification feature. Leaves are alternate and odd-pinnate. Leaflets are nearly entire, but may have a few teeth. Foliage color is a deep, glossy green. The entire leaf margins and the winged rachis are normally all that is needed to identify this plant.

Winged Sumac (Shining Sumac)

153

Buds are not hairy, and the terminal bud is absent. Twigs are not as stout and vigorous as the smooth sumac. Twigs are often minutely pubescent.

Flowers are polygamous or dioecious, greenish, and flower in June or July. Flowers are borne in terminal panicles. Fruits are crimson and ripen in September or October. The terminal fruits are deeper red and not as showy as the smooth sumac.

Smooth Sumac—*Rhus glabra*

This species is closely related to the staghorn sumac. The smooth sumac is the most widespread sumac in Ohio and is found in the west central part of Ohio where staghorn sumac is uncommon. The smooth sumac is smaller in statue than the staghorn sumac. The fall color is outstanding and is the most attractive of the sumacs.

The leaves are alternate, 16–24 inches (41–61 cm) long. The odd-pinnate leaves have 11–25 oblong to lanceolate leaflets with toothed (serrate) margins. Leaf stalks are glabrous (not hairy). The rachis (axis bearing the leaflets) is not winged.

The twigs are smooth and lack the hairy velvet covering of the staghorn sumac. Buds are hairy, and the terminal bud is absent. Twigs are stout and vigorous.

The greenish, dioecious flowers appear in June and July and are borne in terminal panicles. Fruit is borne in terminal panicles and is scarlet in color. The fruit ripens in August or September and is showy well into the winter.

Staghorn Sumac—*Rhus typhina*

The staghorn sumac, also called velvet sumac, is the largest of the native sumacs. Under favorable conditions, it reaches heights of 35 feet and a trunk diameter of 8 inches. The staghorn sumac is found from New Brunswick, Canada, to Minnesota, south to Georgia and Alabama. It oc-

Staghorn Sumac

curs in most areas of Ohio, with fertile, dry uplands as its favorite home. It is common on abandoned fields and along fence rows. It is highly prized for its autumn foliage and the coloration of its fruit.

The leaves are alternate, and 16–24 inches (41–61 cm) long. The odd-pinnate leaves have 11–31 lanceolate leaflets with toothed (serrate) margins. Leaf stalks are hairy.

The twigs are stout, clumsy, and covered with a dense coating of velvety hairs. Twigs have conspicuous lateral buds but lack terminal buds. The buds are small, round, and hairy. Leaf scars are U-shaped and contain three groups of small, greenish bundle scars. Twigs contain a wide, yellowish-brown pith and yield a milky sap when cut or bruised.

The dioecious flowers are small, greenish-yellow, and appear in June or early July. Flowers are borne in pyramidal panicles, 5–12 inches (13–30½ cm) long and 4–6 inches (10–15 cm) broad. The fruit is a small, pubescent, crimson drupe arranged in conspicuous, red seed heads 5–8 inches (13–20 cm) long and 4–6 inches (10–15 cm) broad.

The bark on old trunks is rough and dark brown. On younger trunks it is smooth, thin, and covered with numerous yellowish-brown dots (lenticels). The wood is soft, brittle, rather satiny to touch, orange-colored, and streaked with green.

Staghorn Sumac

155

Poison Sumac

Poison Sumac—*Rhus vernix*

The poison sumac is also called swamp sumac and differs from the other sumacs in that it produces ivory white fruit, as does poison ivy. The poison sumac is found from Ontario, Canada, to Minnesota, and south to Florida and Louisiana. This small tree is rare in Ohio, occurring in Geauga, Cuyahoga, Wayne, Wyandot, Licking, Fairfield, and a few other counties. Swamps, low grounds, and moist slopes are its favorite home. This tree is one of our most poisonous plants. Some people are immune from its attack, while others are highly susceptible. A rash is the most common symptom for this plant, as it is for poison ivy, which is closely related.

The leaves are alternate, odd-pinnate, and 7–14 inches (18–35½ cm) long with 7–13 leaflets. The leaflets are 3–4 inches (7½–10 cm) long and narrowly egg-shaped. Foliage is dark green and shiny above but paler on lower surface. Leaf margins are smooth (entire). The primary leaflet stem (rachis) is not winged.

The flowers appear in June or July. The pollen-bearing and seed-producing flowers occur on different trees. They are small, yellowish-green, and arranged in drooping panicles. The fruit is a small, round, glossy, ivory-white drupe and arranged in loose, drooping clusters that mature in September.

The twigs are stout, orange-brown, smooth, and glossy. The buds are purplish, about ⅕ inch (5 mm) long and sharp-pointed. The wood is soft, brittle, coarse-grained, and light yellow. The bark is smooth, somewhat streaked, light to dark gray, and marked with elongated dots (lenticels).

Cotinus — Smoketree

Smoketrees are deciduous shrubs or small trees with yellow wood. Buds have several scales. Leaves are alternate, entire margined, and have long, slender petioles. Flowers are polygamous or dioecious. Fruit is a drupe. Fruiting panicles bear numerous greenish or purplish hairs.

Key to *Cotinus* Species

I Leaves are quite oval and have entire leaf margins. Leaves are 1¾–3¾ inches (4½–9½ cm) long and have petioles that are more than 1 inch (25 mm) long. It is a shrubby plant or small tree growing to 15 feet. Flowers are yellowish and bloom in June and July. Fruit has long, spreading, purplish or greenish hairs and matures in July and August.

Cotinus coggygria— Common Smoketree

Description of Species

Common Smoketree—*Cotinus coggygria*

An introduced shrub from Europe and Asia, the smoke tree usually grows to 10–15 feet high with a widespreading, bushy crown. When the bark is stripped from branches and twigs, the wood is yellow with a strong-smelling, juicy sap. This ornamental shrub is usually planted as a specimen for its peculiar fruiting effect. This tree has escaped cultivation in disturbed sites but does not appear to be a threat to native vegetation.

Leaves are alternate, entire-margined, and have long, slender petioles. Foliage is oval and has entire leaf margins. Leaves are 1¾–3¾ inches (4½–9½ cm) long and have petioles that are more than 1 inch (25 mm) in length. Foliage is light green to wine (in named cultivars) and smooth.

Flowers are polygamous or dioecious. Flowers are yellow and borne in loose, terminal panicles during June and July. Fruiting panicles are 6–8 inches (15–20 cm) long and contain numerous sterile pedicels furnished with long, spreading purple or green hairs that have the appearance of a hazy smoke, or thin filmy veil covering the foliage when in full bloom. The fruit is a drupe and matures in July and August. The terminal seed head retains its ornamental characteristics into the winter.

Buds are dark, quite small, and have several scales. Wood is distinctively yellow. The plant is too small to have value for lumber.

Common Smoketree

Euonymus — Euonymus

Euonymus that are native to Ohio are deciduous shrubs or small trees. There are also evergreen forms used in the landscape. Twigs are often four-angled. Buds are small with imbricate scales. Leaves are opposite and toothed. Flowers are small and usually perfect. Fruit is a two- to five-celled capsule with seeds enclosed usually in an orange aril, similar to the bittersweet which is closely related.

Key to *Euonymus* Species

I. Leaves are 1½–4¾ inches (4–12 cm) long and pubescent (soft hairy) beneath. Flowers are purple and bloom in May and June. Fruits are scarlet and contain a scarlet seed that ripens in October. This small tree reaches a height of 25 feet.

Euonymus atropurpureus—Wahoo

Description of Species

Wahoo (Burningbush)—*Euonymus atropurpureus*

Wahoo is native to Ohio and is a deciduous shrub or small tree, growing 10–25 feet high. It is normally found growing in fertile soils and rich woodlands. Wahoo is a beautiful ornamental shrub when grown for fall coloring and the attractive, scarlet fruit. The fruit is reported to be poisonous. There are evergreen forms of euonymus used in the landscape.

Leaves are simple, greenish-yellow, finely toothed, and sharply pointed. Opposite leaves are 1½–4¾ inches (4–12 cm) long and pubescent (soft hairy) beneath. Fall color is yellow to scarlet and showy. Buds are small with imbricate scales. Branches and twigs are green with white stripes. Twigs are four-angled.

Flowers are brown to purple, small, and borne on slender stalks. Flowers bloom in May and June. Fruit is a four-lobed, fleshy fruit pod that turns a brilliant scarlet color in autumn. When the fruit opens, it exposes the scarlet aril covering the true seed.

Acer — Maple

Maples are deciduous trees with winter buds bearing several overlapping scales or two uniform, valvate scales. Leaves are opposite and lobed, toothed, or pinnately compound. Flowers are bisexual or have unisexual flowers on the same or different plants. Fruit is a schizocarp that breaks into a two-winged, flattened samara.

Key to *Acer* Species

    I. Leaves are pinnately compound. Side buds are hidden. Leaflets are three to five, rarely seven to nine, with coarsely serrate margins. Leaflets are 2–4 inches (5–10 cm) long. Buds are whitish and pubescent. Twigs are often glaucous. Flowers are yellow-green and emerge before the foliage in March or April. Fruits mature in September in pendant racemes.

          Acer negundo—Boxelder

   II. Leaves are simple and lobed.
      A. Stipules are present. Leaves are usually three-lobed but are occasionally five-lobed and 4–5 ½ inches (10–14 cm) wide. Foliage is dull green above and yellow-green below. Lenticels on twigs are large and warty. Mature bark is dark and deeply furrowed. Flowers are yellow-green and bloom in April. Fruit has wings that are nearly parallel and matures in September. Fall foliage color is yellow.

          Acer saccharum nigrum—Black Maple

    AA. Stipules are absent.
       Ⅰ. Margins of lobes are entire except for points at the tips.
          a. Lobes are blunt or rounded at the tips. Leaves are three- to five-lobed and 2–4 inches (5–10 cm) long and equally wide. Foliage is dull green above and hairy beneath. Petioles of the leaves and young twigs have milky sap. Flowers are yellow-green and bloom in May. Fruits have horizontally spreading wings that mature in August or September. Fall foliage is a poor yellow.

              Acer campestre—Hedge (English) Maple

         aa. Lobes taper and are pointed at the tips.
           i. Ovate buds are large and either red or greenish-red with two to three pairs of bud scales. Petioles and young twigs yield a milky sap. Leaves have five lobes and are 4–7 inches (10–18 cm) wide and not quite as long. Foliage color is bright green above and shiny beneath. Flowers are greenish-yellow and bloom in April or May. Fruit has horizontally spreading wings that mature in September or October. Fall foliage color is yellow.

              Acer platanoides—Norway Maple

ii. Buds are smaller than Norway maple and more pointed with six to 10 pairs of scales. Leaves are three- to five-lobed and 3¼–5½ inches (8½–14 cm) long and wide. Foliage is green above and below and occasionally has a few coarse teeth. Flowers are greenish-yellow, maturing before the foliage in April. Fruit has slightly divergent wings maturing in September. Fall foliage color is yellow, orange, or scarlet and quite showy.

Acer saccharum—Sugar Maple

I I. Margins of lobes are regularly toothed.
   a. Winter buds have two outer, valvate scales.
      i. Larger branches are white- or light green-striped. Leaves are three-lobed at the apex and 4¾–7¼ inches (12–18 cm) long. Foliage is bright green. Flowers are yellow and bloom in May or June. Fruit has spreading wings maturing in September. Fall foliage color is yellow.

Acer pensylvanicum—Striped Maple

      ii. Branches are green and not striped. Twigs, as well as the petioles and midribs of leaves, are pubescent (hairy). Leaves are three-lobed and rarely five-lobed, 2¼–4¾ inches (6–12 cm) long, and yellowish-green above and hairy beneath. Flowers are greenish-yellow and bloom in June. Fruit has wings diverging at right angles and matures in September. Fall color ranges from yellow to scarlet.

Acer spicatum—Mountain Maple

   aa. Winter buds have imbricate (overlapping) scales.
      i. Buds are large and green with few scales. Foliage is greenish-white beneath and dark green, rough, and glabrous above. Leaves are five-lobed, and 3¼–6½ inches (8½–16½ cm) long and wide. Flowers are yellowish-green and borne in May. Fruit has wings spreading at acute or right angles. Fruit matures in August to September, persisting over the winter. Fall foliage color is greenish-yellow and not showy.

Acer pseudoplatanus—Planetree (Sycamore) Maple

ii. Buds are smaller, more pointed, and have more scales than sycamore maple. Leaves are white beneath.

A). Leaves are lobed more than halfway to midrib. Sinuses are U-shaped and the leaves are deeply five-lobed. Leaves are 3¼–5½ inches (8½–14 cm) across, bright green above, and silvery-white beneath. Crushed twigs emit a rank odor. Flowers are greenish-yellow to red and emerge before the foliage in February or March. Fruits have divergent, curved wings and mature in May or June. Fall foliage color is chartruse to yellow.

Acer saccharinum (dasycarpum)—Silver Maple

AA). Leaves are lobed with sinuses less than half way to midrib. Sinus is V-shaped. Leaves have three to five lobes and are 2½–4 inches (6–10 cm) long, medium green, and shiny above and bloomy or paler beneath. Crushed twigs do not emit a rank odor. Flowers are yellow to red, and appear during March and April. Fruits have wings spreading at a narrow angle and ripen in May or June. Fall foliage color is yellow to scarlet and quite showy.

Acer rubrum—Red Maple

Description of Species
Hedge (English) Maple—
Acer campestre

Hedge maple is an ornamental tree introduced from Europe and Asia. The tree is medium-sized and reaches heights of 35–50 feet. The tree is often as broad as it is tall with a broad-headed crown and spreading branches.

Branches and twigs are slender and often covered with corky layers of bark. Buds are smaller than Norway maple and more rounded. Margins of the bud scales often have white hairs. Twigs are a rich brown.

Opposite leaves are three- to five-lobed and are 2–4 inches (5–10 cm) long and equally wide. Margins of the lobes are entire and rounded at the tips. Foliage is dark green above and hairy beneath. Petioles of the leaves and young twigs have milky sap. Stipules are absent.

Flowers are yellow-green and bloom in May. Fruits have horizontally spreading wings that mature in August or September. Fall foliage is a poor yellow.

162

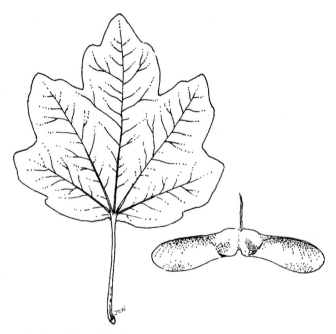

Hedge (English) Maple

Boxelder (Ash-Leaf Maple)—*Acer negundo*

The boxelder is a rapid-growing tree when young. It is found throughout the state on lowlands and in rich soils. It is a tree of medium size, rarely exceeding 24 inches in diameter, and 60–70 feet in height. It has been planted for shade because of its rapid growth. Boxelder's disease sensitivity ensures that it is not long-lived. It is a prolific seed producer, but seedlings are destroyed by grazing and cultivating.

The opposite leaves are odd-pinnate with three to five (rarely seven) leaflets. Foliage is smooth, lustrous, and green with coarsely serrate leaf margins. The leaflets are 2–4 inches (5–10 cm) long by 1–2 inches (2½–5 cm) wide, making the whole leaf 5–8 inches (13–20 cm) in length. This is the only native maple with pinnately compound leaves.

Buds are white and pubescent. Side buds are hidden. Twigs are often glaucous and encircled by the stipular scar. The bark on young branches is smooth and green to purple in color. On older trees it is thin, grayish to light brown, and deeply divided.

Boxelder (Ash-Leaf Maple)

Flowers are yellowish-green and emerge before the foliage in March or April. Fruit matures in September in pendant racemes. The seed is a samara, or winged key, similar to that of a sugar maple, only larger. It ripens in late summer or early fall. The wood is soft, light, weak, close-grained, and decays readily in contact with moisture. It is used occasionally for fuel and pulpwood.

Striped Maple (Moosewood)—*Acer pensylvanicum*

The striped maple is a small tree similar to the mountain maple but is usually larger in height and trunk diameter. It is an attractive small tree in autumn with orange and scarlet leaves, and in the winter the light green stripes stand out conspicuously. This tree is native to Ohio, but is now very rare and reported as native only in Ashtabula County.

Opposite leaves are broad and roundish with three lobes near the point. Leaves are 4¾–7¼ inches (12–18½ cm) long and bright green in color. Leaf margins are regularly toothed.

Winter buds have two outer, valvate scales. Twigs are green and glabrous. Bark on larger branches is smooth, green, and has characteristic stripes with light green or white lines.

Flowers are yellow in pendulous clusters and bloom in May or June. Fruit has spreading wings and matures in September. Fall foliage color is yellow to scarlet and showy.

163

Norway Maple—*Acer plantanoids*

The Norway maple was one of the most popular street trees in the United States in the '60s and '70s. There are very few Ohio towns and cities in which this tree is not found. It originated in Europe where it is native from Norway to Switzerland. It is hardy, retains its leaves longer than the native maples, and endures the smoke, dust, and drought of the city, though it is susceptible to verticillium wilt and girdling roots.

The opposite leaves resemble those of the sugar maple but are deeper green in color and firmer in texture. Leaves have five-pointed lobes and are 4–7 inches (10–18 cm) wide and not quite as long. One characteristic by which it can always be distinguished is the presence of milky sap in the leaf stalks. If pressed or twisted, the leaf stalks always yield a few drops of milky sap. Foliage color is bright green above and shiny beneath, except for the horticultural color variants that include wine, golden, and variegated forms. Fall foliage color is yellow for the green-foliaged forms.

Buds are large (¼ inch [6 mm]) and red or greenish-red with two to three pairs of bud scales; they are a sure means of identification in the winter. Buds are rounded rather than acute-tipped.

In early spring, the yellow to chartruse flowers are arranged in 3-inch (7½ cm) diameter clusters along the twigs. Flowers are borne in April or May. This maple has the most attractive flowers of all maples.

164

Norway Maple

Flowers are showy since they bloom before the foliage emerges. Fruit has horizontally spreading wings that mature in September or October.

Several different horticultural selections are marketed for characteristics such as form and leaf color. Among the most prominent of these cultivars is 'Crimson King,' which is a Norway maple with purple summer foliage. 'Columnare' is a plant with a narrow, upright form when it is young, although it begins to broaden with age. 'Schwedleri' has bronzy spring foliage color and deep green summer foliage. It is longer lived than most Norway maples.

Planetree (Sycamore) Maple—*Acer pseudoplatanus*

A medium-sized tree usually 40–50 feet in height, the planetree is occasionally used for shade and ornamental purposes. This tree was introduced from northern Europe and has difficulty with the warm summers in Ohio. A number of cultivars have been introduced and are marketed for foliage color. This tree is inferior to the Norway maple and generally not suited for Ohio conditions except within a few miles of Lake Erie.

Winter buds have imbricate (overlapping) scales. Buds are large (¼ inch [6 mm]) and green with few scales. Bark on twigs and branches is smooth.

Foliage is greenish-white beneath and dark green, rough, and glabrous above. Leaves are sycamore-like, five-lobed, and 3¼–6½ inches (8½–16½ cm) long and wide. Lobes have coarsely toothed margins. Leaves are dark green above and smooth or slightly hairy on veins. Fall foliage color is greenish-yellow and not showy.

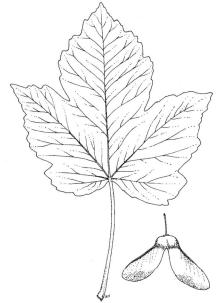

Planetree (Sycamore) Maple

165

The perfect flowers are yellowish-green and hang on stalks 4–5 inches (10–13 cm) long. Flowers emerge in May after the foliage is out. Fruit has wings spreading at acute or right angles. Fruit hangs in showy chains and matures in August or September. Fruit frequently persists over the winter. The samara are smaller than the Norway maple.

Red Maple—*Acer rubrum*

The red maple is widely distributed through the state, although it is much more common in the acidic soil regions of Ohio. It is usually a medium-sized tree with a moderate growth rate.

The bark is smooth and light gray on young- and intermediate-aged stems, while mature bark is dark gray and rough. Crushed twigs do not emit a rank odor as does the silver maple. Twigs are reddish and have rounded, oblong, vegetative buds. Floral buds are globose and conspicuous, since they are borne in clusters. Lower branches tend to sweep upward.

Leaves have three to five lobes and are 2½–4 inches (6–10 cm) long. The leaves have saw-toothed margins, and the lobes are separated by sharp and angular sinuses that extend less than half way to the midrib. The upper surface of the mature leaves is medium green, and the lower surface is white, partly covered with pale down. In autumn, the leaves predominately turn brilliant shades of red but also turn orange and yellow.

The dioecious, red flowers are borne in dense clusters and appear in March or April before the leaves; the buds turn a deep red sometime before they open. Male trees can

Red Maple

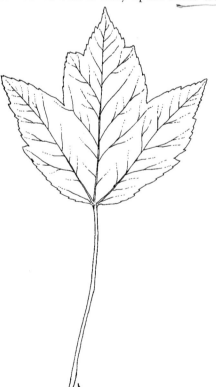

be planted if you do not want fruit. Fruits have wings spreading at narrow angles and ripen in May or June. The fruit consists of pairs of winged seeds, or keys, ½–1 inch (13–25 mm) in length on long, drooping stems. Fruit color ranges from red to green, becoming tan when mature.

The wood is commercially known as soft maple and is heavy, close-grained, rather weak, and light brown color. It is used in the manufacture of furniture, turnery, woodenware, and fuel. Red maple is inferior to black and sugar maple for syrup.

The species makes an excellent suburban or rural landscape tree in acid soil regions of the state. Numerous cultivars are available and are marketed based on fall color and habit. This tree has an acid soil requirement and is intolerant of wounding. With red maples, manganese deficiencies are common in neutral to alkaline soils and are difficult to correct due to the limestone parent material of many Ohio soils.

Silver Maple—*Acer saccharinum (dasycarpum)*

The silver or soft maple is most common on moist land and along streams. It attains heights of 100 feet or more and diameters over 3 feet. It usually has a short trunk which divides into a number of large, ascending limbs. These again subdivide, and small branches droop but turn upward at the tips. The silver maple grows rapidly and has widely been planted as a shade tree. The urban-tolerance of the silver maple makes it the longest-lived of the maples in urban settings. It has been over-planted and should not be planted where maples constitute more than 20 percent of the tree canopy.

The simple leaves are opposite on the stem, 3¼–5½ inches (8–14 cm) across, bright green above, and silvery-white beneath. Leaves are lobed more than half way to midrib. Sinuses are U-shaped and the leaves are deeply five-lobed. The leaf margin is strongly toothed. Fall foliage color is chartruse to yellow and less showy than the red maple.

Silver Maple

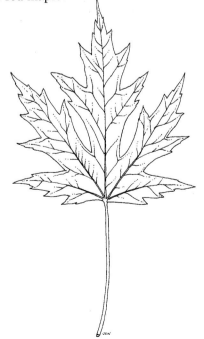

167

Silver

The buds are rounded, red or reddish-brown, blunt-pointed, and generally like those of the red maple. Clusters of globose floral buds are also present on silver maple. On the young twigs the bark is smooth and varies in color from red to a yellowish-gray. Crushed twigs emit a rank odor. The bark on the old stems is dark gray and broken into long flakes.

The flowers appear in February or March, before the leaves, in dense clusters and are of a greenish-yellow or reddish-yellow color. This may be the first native tree to flower, although the flowers are not showy. Fruits have divergent and curved wings that mature in May or June. It consists of a pair of winged seeds, or key, with wings 1–2 inches (2½–5 cm) long on slender, flexible stems about an inch (25 mm) long. Fruit can be a litter problem, since they are borne in great numbers. There are no male trees as this tree can have some perfect flowers.

The wood is soft, weak, even textured, rather brittle, easily worked, and decays readily when exposed to the elements. It is used for furniture, fuel, and pulpwood. Like the red maple, it is sold as soft maple and is inferior to the sugar and black maples as a source of maple syrup.

Sugar Maple—*Acer saccharum*

The sugar maple is generally distributed in Ohio, but is most abundant in the northeastern area. In Ohio, it occurs in pure stands associated with beech, producing the famous sugar bushes of this area. In Geauga County it reaches its best development. The tree attains a height of more than 100 feet and a diameter of 3 feet or more. It is generally a slow-growing tree. In the open, sugar maples have a symmetrical crown. It is extensively planted as a shade tree, although it is urban intolerant and should not be used in tree lawns.

The simple, opposite leaves are three- to five-lobed and 3¼–5½ inches (8½–14 cm) long and wide. The sinuses (division between the lobes) are rounded. The leaves are medium green on the

168

Sugar Maple

upper surface and lighter green beneath. In the autumn, leaves turn to brilliant shades of dark green, scarlet, orange, and yellow.

The bark on young trees is light gray to brown and rather smooth, but as the tree grows older, it breaks up into long irregular plates which vary from light gray to almost black. The twigs are smooth (glabrous) and reddish-brown in color. The winter buds are smaller than Norway maple and sharp-pointed with six to 10 pairs of scales.

The flowers are yellowish-green, on long stalks, and appear with the leaves in April. Male and female flower clusters appear on the same tree. The fruit, which ripens in September, consists of a two-winged key. The two wings are nearly parallel, about 1 inch (25 mm) in length, and each half contains a seed. The seed is easily carried by the wind.

The wood is hard, heavy, strong, close-grained, and light brown in color. It is known commercially as hard maple and is used in the manufacture of flooring, furniture, shoe lasts, and a great variety of novelties. This is the principal tree to be tapped for maple syrup.

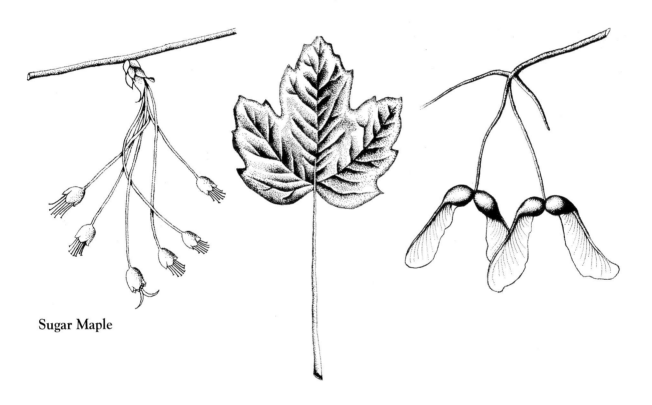

Sugar Maple

Black Maple—*Acer saccharum nigrum*

Black maple is now acknowledged to be an ecotype of the sugar maple. It is distributed generally over the state and more commonly found along streams and broad flood plains, not on the uplands where sugar maple is more common. It is more abundant in the southern part of the state.

The mature bark of the older specimens is deeply furrowed and much darker than the common sugar maple. Lenticels on twigs are large and warty. Year-old twigs are light brown with stipular scars that nearly encircle the twig.

The simple, opposite leaves are a rich, deep green color above with entire wavy margins. Leaves are usually three-lobed but are occasionally five-lobed and are 4–5½ inches (10–14 cm) long and wide. Foliage is dull green above and pale, yellowish-green below. When mature, the leaves have a drooping appearance. The stem of the leaf is enlarged at the base and surrounded by a winged appendage called a stipule. Fall foliage color is yellow.

Flowers are yellowish-green and bloom in April prior to the emergence of the foliage. Fruit is a samara with wings that are nearly parallel. The fruit matures in September.

Commercially, the lumber has the same uses as the sugar maple, and the tree is also a source of maple syrup. This tree may be better adapted as a landscape specimen than sugar maple in Ohio.

Mountain Maple—*Acer spicatum*

A small tree or shrub not over 30 feet in height, the mountain maple is the second of the striped maples. These are forest-understory trees more commonly found in cooler areas. A rare native tree usually confined to the lake area of the northeastern part of Ohio and the cool coves of eastern Ohio, the mountain maple is often associated with the hemlock. Mountain maple is also found in Clifton Gorge in Greene County.

Leaves are three-lobed, rarely five-lobed, 2½–4¼ inches (6–12 cm) long, yellowish-green above, and hairy beneath. Leaf margins have coarse, irregular teeth, and usually have fine hairs beneath with smooth surface above. Foliage is light to yellowish-green in color.

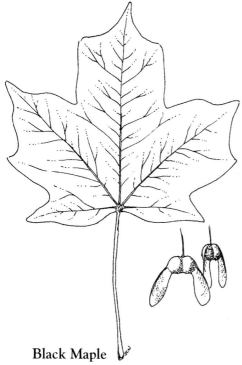

Black Maple

Winter buds have two outer, valvate scales. Twigs, as well as the petioles and midribs of leaves, are pubescent. The color of young bark is green and does not have stripes.

Flowers are greenish-yellow and open in June. Fruit has wings that diverge at right angles and mature in September. Fall color ranges from yellow to scarlet and can be quite showy.

Aesculus — Buckeye, Horsechestnut

Buckeyes and horsechestnuts are deciduous trees with large winter buds having several pairs of outer scales. Leaves are opposite, long-petioled, and palmately compound with five to nine toothed leaflets. Flowers are borne in upright, many-flowered panicles and are showy. Fruit is a large, fleshy nut.

Key to *Aesculus* Species

I. Winter buds are sticky and resinous. The five to seven leaflets are 4–10 inches (10–25 cm) long. Buds are larger and more sticky than others in the genus. Flowers are white, spotted, or tinged yellow and purple, in panicles up to 12 inches (30½ cm) long. The blooms are borne in May or June. Fruits are prickly and mature in September.

   Aesculus hippocastanum—Common Horsechestnut

II. Winter buds are not sticky or resinous.
   A. Five leaflets are 3¼–4¾ (8–12 cm) long. This is a medium-sized tree reaching 35–50 feet. Flowers are greenish-yellow and bloom in May. Fruits are prickly and mature in September

   Aesculus glabra—Ohio Buckeye

   AA. Five leaflets are 4–6 inches (10–15 cm) long. Sweet buckeye is a large tree reaching 65 to 100 feet. Flowers are yellow and bloom in May or June. Fruits do not have prickles and mature in September.

Aesculus octandra—Yellow Buckeye (Sweet Buckeye)

Description of Species
Ohio Buckeye—*Aesculus glabra*

The Ohio buckeye is the state tree and is common throughout Ohio. It may reach a height of 60–70 feet and a diameter of 18–24 inches (41–61 cm) but is usually smaller. The trunk is usually short, limby, and knotty. The crown is generally open and is made up of small, spreading branches.

The leaves are palmately compound, opposite on the stem, and contain five or more leaflets. The leaflets are 3¼–4¾ (8½–12 cm) long. Leaves are generally like those of the yellow buckeye though smaller and fetid. The leaves usually turn yellow and fall early in the autumn. Sometimes the fall color is a soft orange and quite attractive.

Twigs are orange-brown to reddish-brown in color. Winter buds are not sticky. The bark is light gray, but on old trees it is divided into flat scales which make the stem of the tree rough. The bark is ill-smelling when bruised.

Ohio Buckeye

171

The flowers are greenish-yellow to cream-colored and appear in clusters 5–8 inches (13–20 cm) long during April or May. The fruit is regularly rounded, pale brown, and generally thin-walled. Upon breaking into two to three valves, the bright, shiny, mahogany-colored seeds are disclosed. Fruits are prickly and mature in September.

In 1818, F. Michaux described the Ohio Buckeye or American horsechestnut in *North American Sylva, Vol. II*, page 218, saying, "It is unknown in the Atlantic part. I have found it only beyond the mountains and particularly on the banks of the Ohio where it is common. It is called 'Buckeye' by the inhabitants but as the name has been given to the Yellow Buckeye (*lutea*), I have called it 'Ohio Buckeye.'" This was the origin of the name "Ohio Buckeye."

The wood is light, soft, weak, and decays rapidly when exposed. It is used for artificial limbs, paper pulp, and occasionally for lumber. The wood is also used for fuel.

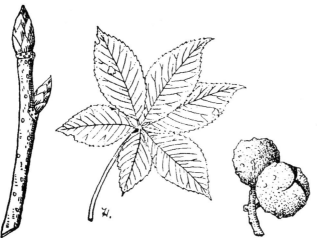

Ohio Buckeye

Common Horsechestnut— *Aesculus hippocastanum*

The horsechestnut has been carried by man from its original home in the mountains of Greece over a considerable part of the civilized world. It is a sturdy, rapidly growing tree now found in every state. The tree is quite urban-tolerant and long-lived in urban situations but is disfigured by a leaf-blotch disease.

The leaves are opposite, palmately compound, and have five to seven leaflets. The leaflets are 4–10 inches (10–25 cm) long and

Common Horsechestnut

about 2 inches (5 cm) wide. The leaflets are inversely egg-shaped and arranged in a fanlike form.

The flowers appear in May or June and are white with throats dotted with yellow and purple. The floral panicle is arranged in an upright cluster between 8–12 inches (20-30½ cm) high. The fruit is a leathery, round capsule about 2 inches (5 cm) across, roughened with spines, containing one to three shiny brown nuts. The nut closely resembles the Ohio buckeye.

The bark is dark brown, and breaks up into thin plates which peel off slowly. The twigs are stout, reddish-brown, smooth, obscurely dotted with breathing pores, and marked with large, horseshoe-like leaf scars, each with five to seven groups of bundle scars.

The buds are large, varnished, reddish-brown, and very resinous. This characteristic distinguishes the tree from the yellow buckeye and Ohio buckeye which have non-resinous buds. Buds are larger and more sticky than others in the genus. The wood is soft, light, weak, and white.

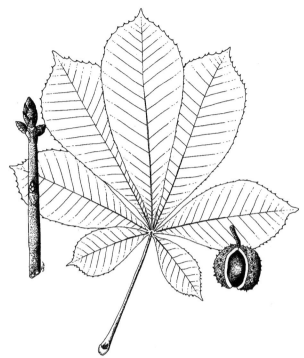

Common Horsechestnut

Yellow (Sweet) Buckeye—*Aesculus octandra*

The yellow buckeye ranges from western Pennsylvania through southern Ohio, Indiana, and Illinois, to Iowa and Oklahoma, and south to Georgia and Texas. It is confined to southern Ohio, extending northward to Monroe and Fairfield counties. Rich bottom lands and lower slopes are its favorite home. It never occurs in pure stands, but is usually found in mixtures with other hardwoods.

The yellow buckeye is also called sweet buckeye and is the largest member of this interesting tree group. It can reach a height of 110 feet and a diameter of 4 feet. Its leaves, flowers, fruit, bark, twigs, and buds resemble those of the Ohio buckeye, but it is a more massive tree.

Five leaflets are 4–6 inches (10–15 cm) long. The leaves are opposite, palmately compound, and have five, and sometimes seven, leaflets. The entire lower leaf surface is more permanently pubescent in this tree than in the Ohio buckeye. Fall color is an attractive, soft orange. Foliage is resistant to the leaf-blotch problems experienced by Ohio buckeye.

Yellow (Sweet) Buckeye

173

The buds are non-resinous. The sticky-bud characteristic is very helpful in distinguishing this tree from the horsechestnut, which has very resinous buds. It can be distinguished from Ohio buckeye by its smoother and lighter-colored bark as well as its larger size.

Flowers are yellow and bloom in May or June. The anthers of its flowers remain within the corolla, while those of the Ohio buckeye extend beyond the corolla. Fruits are without prickles and mature in September. The capsule of its fruit contrasts with that of the Ohio buckeye and horsechestnut that is warty or spiny.

The wood is light, soft, weak, and white to pale yellow in color. It is used for paper pulp, woodenware, slack cooperage, artificial limbs, and locally for lumber and interior finishing. In some sections of Ohio, the yellow buckeye is planted as an ornamental tree.

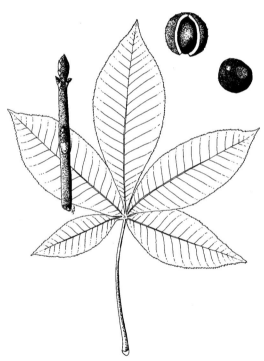

Yellow (Sweet) Buckeye

174

Tilia — Linden

Lindens, or basswoods, are deciduous trees that have large winter buds with few scales. Terminal buds are absent. Leaves are alternate with toothed leaf margins and usually have cordate leaf bases. Flowers are perfect and fragrant. The fruit is distinctive. The clusters of nutlike fruits have a wing adpressed to the pedicel of the fruit cluster.

Key to *Tilia* Species

I. Leaves are 4–7 inches (10–18 cm) long and glossy green above with close, thick, and white or sometimes brown tomentum beneath. Twigs are red or yellowish-brown and glabrous. Flowers are yellow and borne in July.

Tilia heterophylla—Bee Tree Linden

II. Leaves are without thick tomentum beneath the leaf. Leaves are glabrous on veins beneath.

    A. Leaves are 3¼–5¼ inches (8½–14 cm) long. Leaves are glabrous except for axillary tufts of hairs beneath. Twigs are green to red and glabrous. Flowers are yellow and bloom in July.

Tilia americana—American Linden (Basswood)

    AA. Leaves are 1¼–2½ inches (3–6 cm) long. Foliage is glabrous and shiny above and is glabrous beneath as well. Flowers are yellowish-white and open in July.

Tilia cordata—Littleleaf Linden

Description of Species

American Linden (Basswood)—*Tilia americana*

The American linden is found in Canada from New Brunswick to Manitoba, southward to Georgia and Texas, and is common throughout Ohio. Rich, moist bottom lands and hillsides are its favorite haunts. It reaches a height of 70–80 feet and sprouts freely. The suckers can serve as an identification feature in the woods. It is a handsome shade tree, transplants easily, grows rapidly, and produces useful wood.

The leaves are simple, alternate, roundish and 3¼–5¼ inches (8–13 cm) long. Foliage is firm in texture, toothed along the margin, and unequally heart-shaped at the base. Leaves are glabrous or have tufts of rusty hair in axils of veins. Leaves lack the thick tomentum beneath the leaf that characterizes the white linden.

The bark on young stems is smooth and dark gray. On older trunks it becomes thick and clearly furrowed. The twigs are glabrous, shiny, rather stout, often zigzagged, and green to red in color. The buds

American Linden (Basswood)

American Linden (Basswood)

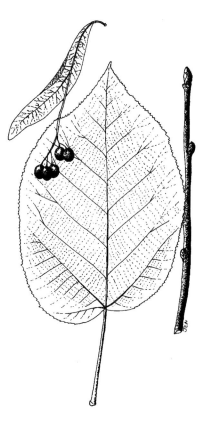

are egg-shaped, two-ranked, stout, blunt-pointed, and usually deep red with three visible bud scales. Terminal buds are absent.

Flowers are perfect, fragrant, and borne in cymes of five to 20. Flowers are yellow and bloom in July. Honeybees are attracted in numbers and may be a concern for some. The axillary peduncle of flowers and fruit are united to a strap-shaped, short-stalked, leaflike bract that allows the seed to be carried by the wind in a helicopter-like fashion. The winged fruit is unique to lindens. The fruits themselves are nutlike berries about the size of a pea and often persist on the tree far into winter.

This is a valuable timber tree. The wood is soft and easily worked. The light-colored wood takes stain well. Lindens are a good source of nectar for honeybees. The honey is especially prized. American linden is valuable as a wildlife tree with hollows in mature trees serving as homes to a variety of wildlife.

Littleleaf Linden—*Tilia cordata*

Littleleaf linden is a smaller tree than the other lindens listed here. This European introduction has a rather formal, round-shaped head. Littleleaf linden is planted in parks, streets, and lawns for ornamental purposes. This is one of the best medium-sized ornamental trees that reaches a height of 50–60 feet.

The foliage is decidedly smaller than American linden and is broader than it is long. Leaves are 1¼–2½ inches (3–6 cm) long. The color of leaves is dark green above and paler green beneath. The leaf shape is rounded with a heart-shaped base, sharply pointed leaf tips, and finely toothed margins. Foliage is glabrous and shiny on both sides of the leaf.

Flowers are perfect and fragrant. Flowers are creamy yellow and bloom in July. The axillary peduncle of flowers and fruit are united to a strap-shaped, short-stalked, leaflike bract that allows the seed to be carried by the wind in a helicopter-like fashion. The winged fruit is unique to lindens. The fruits themselves are nutlike.

Lindens are deciduous trees that have large winter buds with few scales. Terminal buds are absent. Twigs are a soft yellow-brown during the winter.

Wood is soft and weak. Nectar produces the finest honey in Europe by some accounts. Bees are attracted in large numbers and may be a threat to individuals who are sensitive to bee stings.

Littleleaf Linden

White Basswood (Bee Tree Linden)— *Tilia heterophylla*

White basswood is a tree quite similar to American linden with larger leaves and smooth, reddish-brown or dark yellow bark on twigs and branches. It is more southerly in distribution than the American linden and is confined to the southern part of state in the tier of counties bordering the Ohio River. Rich, moist bottom lands and hillsides are its favorite homes. It reaches heights of 70–80 feet and sprouts freely. The suckers can be used as an identification feature in the woods. It is a handsome shade tree, transplants easily, grows rapidly, and produces useful wood.

The simple leaves are 4–7 inches (10–18 cm) long and glossy green above. The leaves are larger than other lindens. The under surfaces of the leaves are covered with a downy, white (sometimes brown) fuzz or a cotton-like mass of hair.

Twigs are red or yellowish-brown and glabrous. Winter buds have only three scales showing. Terminal buds are absent.

Perfect, fragrant flowers are yellow and borne in cymes. The flowers in July are attractive to bees and should be avoided by people who are sensitive to bee stings. The nectar is an excellent source of honey. The axillary peduncle of flowers and fruit are united to a strap-shaped, short-stalked, leaflike bract that allows the seed to be carried by the wind in a helicopter-like fashion. The winged fruit is unique to lindens. The brown fruits themselves are nutlike.

Wood is soft, not strong, and light-colored. It is easily worked in cabinetry. Wounds often lead to cavities in the tree and homes for wildlife.

White Basswood (Bee Tree Linden)

178

Nyssa — Blackgum (Tupelo)

Blackgums are deciduous trees with scaly buds and diaphragmed pith. Leaves are alternate, oval, and have entire leaf margins, but the leaf margins are sometimes slightly toothed. Flowers are either polygamous or dioecious. Fruit is a drupe.

Key To *Nyssa* Species

I. Leaves are 2–4¾ inches (5–12 cm) long. Leaves are glossy above and somewhat bloomy beneath. Buds are imbricate. Flowers are inconspicuous and borne in May or June. Fruit is a blue-black drupe that matures in October.

Nyssa sylvatica—Blackgum (Black Tupelo)

Description of Species

Blackgum (Black Tupelo)—*Nyssa sylvatica*

The blackgum, often call sourgum, has been considered a weed in the forest due to the low value of the lumber in Ohio. In the lowlands it is occasionally found in year-round swamps with elm and in the hills and on dryer slopes with oaks and hickories.

The alternate, simple leaves are 2–4¾ inches (5–12 cm) long. Leaves are glossy, deep green above and somewhat bloomy beneath. Leaves are oval but may be broader near the apex, shiny, and dark green in color. Leaf margins are generally entire but sometimes are slightly toothed. In the fall, the leaves turn a brilliant red.

Buds are imbricate. Twigs have distinctively diaphragmed pith. The bark on young trees is furrowed between flat ridges and gradually develops into quadrangular blocks that are dense, hard, and nearly black.

The green flowers on long, slender stems appear in May or June when the leaves are about one-third grown. Flowers may be polygamous or dioecious, but they are usually of two kinds. The male is borne in many-flowered heads and the female

Blackgum (Black Tupelo)

179

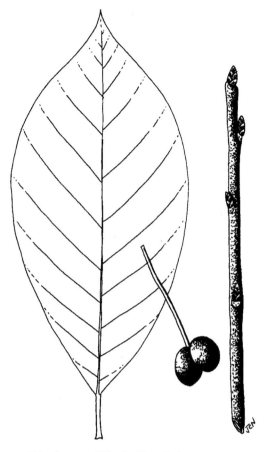

Blackgum (Black Tupelo)

in two- to several-flowered clusters on different trees. The fruit is a dark blue, fleshy drupe, ⅓–⅔ inch (8–17 mm) long, containing a single, hard-shelled seed. They, too, are borne on long stems, two to three in a cluster, and mature in October.

The wood is very tough, cross-grained, and not durable in contact with the soil. The wood is hard to work and warps easily. It is used for crate and basket veneers, rollers, mallets, rough floors, mine trams, pulpwood, and fuel. In the old days, the hollow trunks were used for "bee gums." Tupelo honey is prized in the southern United States.

Black tupelo is one of our most brilliantly colored trees in the fall. Often the coloring starts in late summer and continues until mid-autumn when the trees seem ablaze with brilliant red foliage. For this reason, it can be considered an excellent native tree to plant for both color and ornamental effect. The nursery industry has recently begun to offer this plant in containers, as this plant is difficult to otherwise transplant. This tree requires an acid soil and is not a good landscape subject in the alkaline soils of the till-plains region.

Aralia — Aralia

Aralias are curious, deciduous trees or shrubs that are armed with stout prickles. Branches have large pith and winter buds with few outer scales. Leaves are alternate or pinnate to thrice pinnately compound. Flowers are borne in large, terminal panicles. Fruit is a small, berrylike drupe.

Key to *Aralia* Species

      I. Leaves are alternate and twice pinnately compound. Twigs are spiny. Spines are unbranched, short, and stout. Leaves are 16–30 inches (41–76 cm) or larger with prickles on the upper surface of the rachis. Flowers are white and bloom in August. Fruit is a black drupe that matures in September or October.

Aralia spinosa—Devil's Walkingstick

Description of Species
Devil's Walkingstick (Hercules' Club)—
Aralia spinosa

The devil's walkingstick grows in the moist soil of deep woods and, though usually a shrub, sometimes becomes a tree 30–40 feet in height with a trunk diameter of from 6–8 inches (15–20 cm). It grows rapidly and is sometimes cultivated for ornamentation due to its curious habit.

The trunk branches and leaf stalks are very prickly and the twigs are thick and stout with a large pith. Trunks are sparsely branched. The bark is dark brown with yellow inner bark that is about ⅛ inch (3 mm) thick. The bark is divided by shallow fissures into wide rounded ridges. The bark is sometimes used for medicinal purposes.

The leaves are twice compound, very large, and clustered at the ends of the branches. Leaves are 16–30 inches (41–76 cm) or larger and 2 feet wide. The leaflets are only 2–3 inches (5–7 cm) long and half as wide. Foliage is dark green above and pale beneath. The petiole is about 1½ feet (46 cm) long, enlarged at the base, and clasped to the stem with prickles on all parts of the leaf rachis or stem and even on the mid-veins of the leaflets.

Flowers are white and bloom in August. They are very small and form a terminal panicle which is usu-

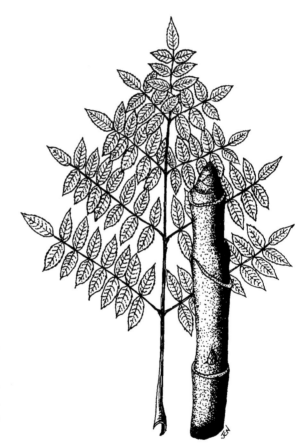

Devil's Walkingstick (Hercules' Club)

ally over 3 feet long. The ⅛ inch (3 mm) in diameter black fruit is fleshy, round, and slightly angled. Fruit is a drupe that matures in September or October.

The wood is light, close-grained, and brown in color, streaked with yellow, with a layer of lighter-colored sapwood of two to three rings. This species is related to ginseng, and the berries and the bark of the roots have medicinal uses. It has been reported from Ashtabula, Summit, Athens, Hocking, Jackson, Preble, Clermont, and Adams counties.

Cornus — Dogwood

Dogwoods are deciduous trees or shrubs with valvate, scaly, and elongated winter buds. Leaves are normally opposite but may be alternate. Leaf margins are entire and have veins that run parallel to the leaf margin. Flowers are white or yellow. The actual flowers are perfect and small; they may have showy bracts. Fruits are drupes.

Key To *Cornus* Species

I. Leaves and buds are opposite. Branching is sympodial, and the side buds may take the lead. Leaves are 3¼–6 inches (8½–15 cm) long. Twigs are green or purple and often have a white bloom. Flower buds are stalked. Flower bracts are showy and either white or pink. The actual flowers are yellow and open in May. Fruit is a red drupe that is borne in clusters and matures between September and November.

Cornus florida—Flowering Dogwood

II. Leaves and buds are alternate. Branching is sympodial, and the side buds may take the lead. Purplish-green branches spread in irregular whorls forming horizontal tiers. Leaves have parallel veins and are 2½–5 inches (6–13 cm) long. Usually, the leaves are crowded at the end of twigs. Flowers are white, small, and open in May or June. Fruit is a bluish-black drupe that ripens in August. This small tree reaches heights of 25 feet.

Cornus alternifolia—Pagoda Dogwood

182

Description of Species
Pagoda (Alternate-Leafed) Dogwood—
Cornus alternifolia

Alternate-leafed dogwood is a shrub or small tree usually less than 20 feet in height. Pagoda dogwood is found growing in rich soils or along fertile flood plains. It is reported throughout Ohio but is not abundant anywhere. This tree is drought sensitive. The name pagoda dogwood is derived from the horizontal branches that reminded someone of the tiers of a pagoda.

Twigs have smooth, purplish-green bark that has a distinct, bitter taste. Leaves and buds are alternate. Branching is sympodial. The side buds may take the lead, thus forming horizontal tiers of branches in spiral whorls.

Leaves are arranged alternately and clustered at the ends of twigs. Leaves have veins that run parallel to the leaf margins and are 2½–5 inches (6–13 cm) long. Foliage is smooth, rather shiny above, and has a faint, hairy covering beneath. Leaf margins are entire to undulate.

Flowers are perfect, small, and white, and they open in May or June after the foliage has expanded. Flowers are borne in flat cymes up to 3 inches (7½ cm) across. Unlike the flowering dogwood, the pagoda dogwood does not have showy bracts. Fruit is a dark, bluish-black drupe with a light bloom and red pedicels. Fruit ripens in August. The fruit is relished by birds, squirrels, and other small mammals and is normally consumed well before fall arrives.

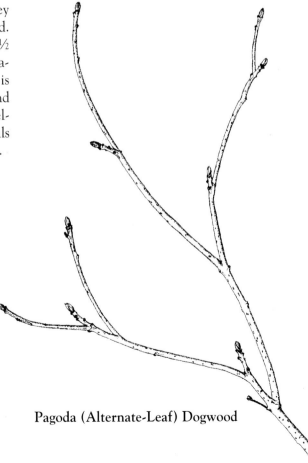

Pagoda (Alternate-Leaf) Dogwood

183

Flowering Dogwood

Flowering Dogwood—*Cornus florida*

The flowering dogwood is found growing mostly in the acid soil regions of the state, usually under the larger forest trees. It is a small tree, usually 15–30 feet high and 6–12 inches in diameter. Occasionally, the tree gets larger with a rather flat-spreading crown and with a short, often crooked, trunk.

The leaves are opposite, ovate, 3¼–6 inches (8½–15 cm) long, and 2–3 inches (5–7½ cm) wide. The leaf has a pointed tip and an entire or undulate leaf margin. Foliage is bright green above and pale green or grayish beneath. The veins of the leaves turn and run parallel to the leaf margin, making dogwood leaves easy to identify.

Branching is sympodial, and the side buds may take the lead. This characteristic results in horizontal branching. Twigs are green or purple and often have a white bloom. Flower buds are stalked and conspicuous during the winter months. The bark is reddish-brown to black and broken into small, four-sided, scaly blocks.

The flowers unfold from the round, conspicuous, gray winter flower buds before the leaves come out. The white or pink flower bracts are showy and often thought to be the petals of the flower. The actual flowers are yellow and borne in a central cluster; they open in May. The fruit is a bright scarlet, berrylike drupe that is ½ inch (13 mm) long and contains a hard nutlet in which there are one to two seeds. Usually several fruits are contained in one head. The fruit is relished by birds, squirrels, and other animals which often eat the fruit before it colors and matures, usually between September and November.

The dogwood, with its masses of early spring bracts, its dark red autumn foliage, and its bright red berries, is probably our most showy native tree. Numerous named cultivars are available in the nursery trade, although most are not cold-hardy in Ohio. Pink and red "flowered" selections are generally not hardy. Since Ohio is at the northwest limits of flowering dogwood's natural range, Ohioans should use locally adapted seed sources of this showy native. A hardy seed source marketed as 'Richland' is available in the nursery industry.

There is a great deal of concern today about the impact of dogwood anthracnose. This disease is causing trouble in the cloud-forest region of the Allegheny Mountains and along the east coast. It is a more likely concern in Ohio in the lake-effect areas of Ohio. While the Chinese dogwood is resistant to anthracnose, it is less cold-hardy than the native flowering dogwood. The bottom line is that the best showy dogwood is still local seed sources of the native flowering dogwood.

The wood is hard, heavy, strong, very close-grained, and brown to red in color. The wood was revered by the fabric mills for spindles.

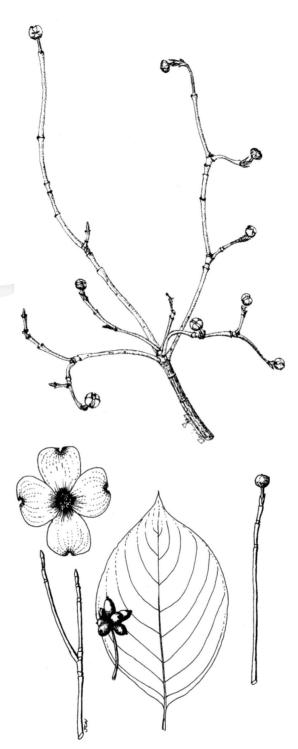

Flowering Dogwood

Oxydendrum — Sourwood

Sourwood is a medium-sized deciduous tree with small, imbricate, winter buds that have three outer scales. Leaves are alternate and ovate to lanceolate in shape with slightly toothed margins. Flower are perfect, showy, and borne in terminal panicles. Fruit is a capsule.

Key to *Oxydendrum* Species

I. Leaves are large, peach-like, and 3¼–8 inches (8½–20 cm) long with finely toothed margins. The petiole is usually less than ⅗ inch (15 mm) long. Flowers are white and open in July or August. Fruit is gray and matures in September or October. Fall foliage color is scarlet.

Oxydendrum arboreum—Sourwood (Sorrel Tree)

Sourwood (Sorrel Tree)

Description of Species
Sourwood (Sorrel Tree)—
Oxydendrum arboreum

The sourwood is a tree of moderate dimensions, 8–12 inches (20–30½ cm) in trunk diameter and 40–60 feet high. It is found only in the southeastern portion of the state, from Fairfield County southward. Sourwood is usually found along ridge tops and upper slopes capped with sandstone, although it thrives on more favored soil sites as well. Large specimens have been observed growing in coves and richer slopes mixed with tuliptree, chestnut oak, hickory, and red oak. Sourwood, sumac, black tupelo, scarlet oak, and sassafras are the major sources of red color fall color in the Ohio landscape.

The simple, alternate leaves are 3¼–8½ inches (8–20 cm) long. Leaves are ovate to lanceolate in shape with slightly toothed margins. The petiole is usually less than ⅗ inch (15 mm) long. Leaves are glabrous, lustrous green on the upper surface, and lighter green and slightly pubescent on the veins beneath. Foliage generally turns a deep crimson in the fall and has a decidedly acid taste.

Winter buds are small and imbricate with three outer scales. The strong, straight first year twigs are often a bright red. The bark is thin, light gray, and divided into narrow, shallow ridges.

The perfect flowers are small, white or cream-colored, and borne in drooping, terminal racemes 5–10 inches (13–25 cm) long. Flowers open in July or August. They provide storehouses of nectar from which bees make excellent honey. The fruit is a conical, dry capsule, ⅓–½ inch (8-13 mm) in length, containing numerous small seeds. Fruit is grayish and matures in September or October. These capsules hang in drooping panicles into the winter.

The wood is heavy, hard, very close-grained, compact, brown in color, and sometimes tinged with red. It is used for turnery, handles, and some other uses.

Sourwood (Sorrel Tree)

187

Diospyros — Persimmon

Persimmons are deciduous trees with buds bearing three outer scales. Terminal buds are absent. Flowers are dioecious. Fruit is a large, juicy berry.

Key to *Diospyros* Species

    I. Leaves are round to elliptic, and 2½–5½ inches (6–14 cm) long. Foliage is glossy, dark green above, and paler beneath. Bark of mature trunks is dark and scaly. Flowers are white and bloom in May or June. Fruit is yellowish-orange and often has a red cheek. Fruit is edible and matures in October or November.

Diospyros virginiana—Common Persimmon

Common Persimmon

Description of Species
Common Persimmon—*Diospyros virginiana*

    The persimmon is found from Rhode Island to Florida and west to Kansas and Texas. It thrives best on the light, sandy soils of the warm south. In Ohio, this tree occurs south of Columbus. It is frequent in the counties drained by the Ohio River. Persimmons rarely exceed 50 feet in height and 18 inches in diameter.

    The simple, alternate leaves are oval to ovate in shape and 2½–5½ inches (6–14 cm) long. Leaves have pointed tips and entire leaf margins. Foliage is glabrous, glossy, dark green above, and paler beneath.

    Terminal buds are absent. The broad, egg-shaped lateral buds are imbricate and have three outer scales. The twigs are reddish-brown with rather large, chambered pith. Lateral buds are marked with half-moon-shaped leaf scars containing only one bundle scar. The mature bark is deeply furrowed and breaks into dark gray to black square blocks separated by furrows that are cinnamon-red along the bottom.

    Flowers are dioecious, yellow to white, and bloom in May or June. Male trees have no fruit, if none is desired. The persimmon is best known by its fruit, which is the largest berry produced by an American forest tree. There is no better way to get acquainted with this tree than to try to eat its fruit before it is ripe. Its harsh taste draws the lips and chokes the throat. It is a red to yellow, pulpy berry 1–1½ inches (25–38 mm) in diameter. The bitterness of the fruit disappears with age and frost action, becoming smooth and sweet as it matures in October or November. It is edible.

    The wood is hard, heavy, and strong. The heartwood is brown to black; the sapwood is wide and white to yellow in color. It is used for golf club heads and shuttles.

Fraxinus — Ash

Ashes are large, deciduous trees with brown or black winter buds having one to two pairs of outer scales. Leaves are opposite and pinnately compound. Flowers are perfect or unisexual. Fruit is a one-seeded nutlet with elongated wings.

Key to *Fraxinus* Species

I. Twigs are pubescent.

    A. Leaves are dark green and glaucous above and pubescent beneath. The seven to nine leaflets are often falcate and have entire leaf margins.

        Fraxinus biltmoreana—Biltmore Ash

    AA. Leaflets usually have toothed margins and are pubescent beneath. There are five to nine leaflets that are lanceolate and not falcate. Leaf scars are half-round and normally straight across the top.

        Fraxinus pennsylvanica—Green Ash

II. Twigs are glabrous and not hairy.

    A. Branches are four-angled. Leaves have seven to 11 short-stalked leaflets.

        Fraxinus quadrangulata—Blue Ash

    AA. Branches are round.

        1. Leaflets are stalked. Leaf scars are half-round. The first pair of lateral buds usually occurs at the base of the terminal bud.

            a. There are four to nine, usually seven, leaflets with entire or slightly toothed margins. Leaf scars are usually notched at the top.

                Fraxinus americana—White Ash

            aa. There are five to nine leaflets with toothed margins. Leaf scars are usually straight at the top.

                Fraxinus pennsylvanica—Green Ash

        11. Leaflets are sessile. Leaf scars are more vertically elliptic than half-round. The first pair of side buds is usually below the terminal bud.

            a. Buds are black. There are seven to 11 leaflets that are villous (long, soft, curved hairs) along the midrib.

                Fraxinus excelsior—European Ash

            aa. Buds are dark brown. There are seven to 11 leaflets that are rusty-woolly along the midrib.

                Fraxinus nigra—Black Ash

Description of Species
White Ash—*Fraxinus americana*

The white ash is found throughout the state, but reaches its best development on the heavy, clay soils in northeastern Ohio. In the southeastern part of Ohio, it is limited to the streams and lower slopes. It reaches an average height of 50–80 feet and a diameter of 2–3 feet, though much larger trees are found in virgin forest. Numerous cultivars are available in the nursery trade. Cultivars are marketed for purple fall color. White ash is drought-sensitive in woods and the landscape and should be avoided in drought-ridden sites.

Leaves are opposite and odd-pinnately compound. The leaves of the white ash are from 8–12 inches (20–30 cm) long and have from five to nine plainly stalked, sharp-pointed leaflets. Leaflets are 3–6 inches (7½–15 cm) long and 1–3 inches (2½–7½ cm) wide. Leaflets have entire or slightly toothed margins and have fewer teeth than green ash. Foliage is dark green and smooth above, and pale green beneath. Fall color ranges from yellow through brown to a deep wine color and may be showy.

Branches are round. Winter buds have one to two pairs of outer scales. Leaf scars are half-round and are usually deeply notched at the top. The first pair of lateral buds usually occurs at the base of the terminal bud. The mature bark varies in color from a light gray to a gray brown. The narrow ridges are separated regularly by deep, diamond-shaped fissures.

The flowers are usually of two kinds on different trees. The male is in dense, reddish-purple clusters while the female is in more open bunches. The fruit of the ash is winged, 1–1½ inches (25–38 mm) long, and resembles the blade of a canoe paddle in outline with

White Ash

the seed at the handle end. The fruits mature in late summer and are distributed effectively by the winds.

The wood of the white ash is extremely valuable because of its toughness and elasticity. It is preferred over all other native woods for small tool handles; athletic implements such as rackets, bats, and oars; and agricultural implements. It is also used extensively for furniture and interior finish. Interestingly, the dead wood of ash loses its strength and becomes dangerously unstable.

Biltmore Ash—*Fraxinus biltmoreana*

The biltmore ash is similar to, but smaller than, the white ash. Distribution is principally in western Ohio and largely confined to the southwestern portion of the state. Some feel that this is a variety of white ash rather than a separate species. Commercially the lumber is marketed in the lumber trade with white ash.

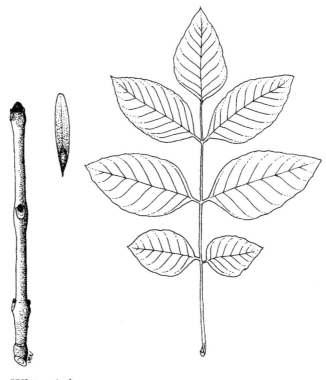

White Ash

Leaves are odd-pinnate with seven to 11 ovate to oval-shaped leaflets. Leaflets are 3½–6 inches (9–15 cm) long. Leaflets are rounded at the base and sharply pointed at the tip. The leaflets are often falcate and have entire or finely toothed leaf margins. Foliage is dark green and smooth above and bluish-white, covered with fine hairs, beneath. The hairs are denser along the veins.

Biltmore ash can be easily separated from white ash by the twigs and stems that are densely covered with fine, soft hairs. Winter buds have one to two pairs of outer scales. The leaf scars are shallowly notched at the top. Twigs are circular in outline. The bark is noticeably furrowed on young trees. As the biltmore ash grows older, the furrows become deeper and the ridges become broader than the white ash.

Flowers are perfect or unisexual and open before the leaves are expanded in April or May. Fruit is a straight, 1-inch (25 mm) samara borne in clusters.

191

European Ash

European Ash—
Fraxinus excelsior

European ash is a smaller tree than the native American white ash and is quite similar to the black ash. As expected, this tree was introduced from Europe and western Asia. A number of cultivars have been introduced in the nursery trades in the United States and Europe. One cultivar has a simple leaf and is more commonly seen. They have not proven serviceable in U.S. landscapes and are rarely used. Lilac and ash borers are problems for this tree.

Leaves are opposite and pinnately compound. There are seven to 11 leaflets that are villous (long, soft, curved hairs) along the midrib. Leaflets are short-stalked or sessile with sharply toothed margins. Foliage is deep green above and lighter green beneath.

Winter buds have one to two pairs of outer scales and are black. Branches are dull gray to dark brownish. Leaf scars are more vertically elliptic than half-round. The first pair of side buds is usually below the terminal bud.

Flowers are perfect or unisexual. Flowers are borne as the foliage begins to emerge in April or May. Fruit is a samara.

Black Ash—*Fraxinus nigra*

Black ash is smaller than the green ash or the white ash and has a more northerly distribution. Since it is a swamp species, it grows naturally in wet places. It is common in northern and southwestern Ohio, becoming rare in southeastern Ohio. Originally in the Black Swamp area of northwestern Ohio, black ash was prominently associated with cottonwood, American elm, soft maple, bur oak, and swamp white oak. The bark is gray and scaly and crumbles when rubbed with the palm of the hand. In dense stands, the tree is from 70–90 feet tall and 10–12 inches in diameter. Open-grown trees are half the height of woodland trees.

Black Ash

Leaves are opposite and odd-pinnately compound. The leaves are dark green and smooth above, and lighter beneath. There are seven to 11 leaflets that are rusty-woolly along the midrib. The leaflets are sessile. Leaf margins have small teeth.

Winter buds have one to two pairs of outer scales. Leaf scars are more vertically elliptic than half-round. The first pair of side buds is usually below the terminal bud. Buds are dark brown, almost black, and are narrower and more pointed than those of the white ash.

Flowers are perfect or unisexual. The fruit is a single key or samara and shaped like a canoe paddle. The seed is almost entirely surrounded by a wing. The end of the wing may be rounded or slightly notched.

The wood is light brown in color and lighter than the white ash, but not as strong. The wood has a decided grain which makes it suitable for furniture and interior finish. The Indians found that by pounding the wood of young stems, they could separate it into layers. The layers were used for baskets. Black ash wood is used for butter tubs, splint boxes, cabinet making, and veneers for baskets.

Green Ash—*Fraxinus pennsylvanica*

Green ash is smaller than white ash and usually does not exceed 60 feet. The tree has a shorter trunk and a rounded, open head. The green ash is found along the streams in all but extremely hilly sections of the state. This tree has spreading branches, an irregular growth habit, and a trunk diameter up to 2 feet. Two varieties are known. The variety *subintegerrima* (green ash) is characterized by glabrous branches and a more easterly range. The variety *lanceolata* (red ash) has pubescent branches and leaf veins, and a more northerly and westerly range.

The leaves are opposite one another on the stem and are odd-pinnately compound with a total length of 10–12 inches (25–30½ cm). There are five to nine stalked leaflets that are lanceolate and not falcate. Foliage is dark to light green. Leaflets usually have toothed margins and may be glabrous or pubescent beneath. Fall color is a clear yellow.

The mature bark is ½ inch (13 mm) or more thick, brown tinged with red, and slightly furrowed or ridged. Twigs and leaf stems may or may not be pubescent. The leaf scar is half-round and normally straight across the top. Winter buds have one to two pairs of outer scales. The twigs are round and ashy gray, marked by pale lenticels and rusty bud-scales.

The flowers are small with the male and female flowers occurring on different trees. Flowers open just prior to leaf expansion in April or May. The fruit is flat, winged, 1–2½ inches (2½–6 cm) long, and ¼–⅓ inches (6–8 mm) wide. The winged portion of the samara extends down past the middle of the seed-bearing portion. The wing is sometimes square or slightly notched at the outer end.

There are a number of named cultivars that are available in the nursery trade. Most green ashes are selected for yellow fall color, male flowers that do not produce fruit, and environmental-tolerance when established. 'Summit' has an oval habit until it reaches 10 inches (25 cm) in trunk diameter. 'Patmore' is distinguished by its cold-tolerance. Green ash must be sprayed when planted in the landscape for one to two years to control ash and lilac borers.

The wood is heavy, hard, rather strong, brittle, and coarse-grained. The light brown heartwood has a rather broad layer of lighter sapwood. The wood is similar to that of the white ash, though not as desirable, and is generally used for the same purposes.

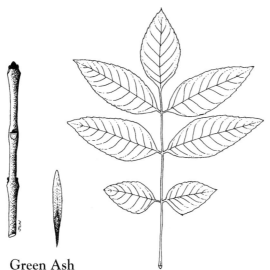

Green Ash

Blue Ash—*Fraxinus quadrangulata*

The blue ash is confined to the limestone soils of western Ohio. It is seldom found in the eastern part of the state. The blue ash ranges from southern Ontario, Canada, to Iowa and south to northern Alabama and Arkansas. The blue ash becomes a large tree, 100 feet in height with a trunk 3 feet in diameter. Only one cultivar is in the nursery trade, and it is very uncommon. This tree's alkaline soil tolerance has not been exploited by our urban communities.

The leaves are opposite, and odd-pinnately compound with a total length of 8–12 inches (20–30½ cm). Leaves have seven to 11 short-stalked leaflets. Leaflets are 2–5 inches (5–13 cm) long and 1–2 inches (2½–5 cm) wide and are more lanceolate in outline than the white ash. Leaflets are acute-tipped and coarsely toothed. The leaves are thick, firm, smooth, yellowish-green above, and paler beneath. The veins, mid ribs, and leaflet stalks are permanently pubescent.

The young twigs afford the most characteristic feature of this species, as they are usually square, sometimes winged, or four-ridged between the leaf bases. This makes it the easiest to recognize of all the native ash trees. Twigs are glabrous. Winter buds have one to two pairs of outer bud scales. The mature bark is ½– ⅔ inches (13–17 mm) thick, light grayish tinged with red, and irregularly divided into large, platelike scales. Macerating the inner bark in water yields the blue dye that gives this tree its name.

The flowers are without petals and appear in clusters when the buds begin to expand. Flowers are perfect or bisexual, thus the blue ash cannot be selected for fruitless trees. The fruit is flattened, oblong, 1–2 inches (2½–5 cm) long, and less than ½ inch (13 mm) wide. The wings of the samara are usually notched at the outer end.

The wood is heavy, hard, and close-grained. The wood is light yellow, streaked with brown, and has a very broad zone of lighter sapwood. It is not distinguished commercially from the wood of other ash trees.

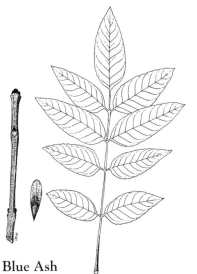

Blue Ash

195

Chionanthus — Fringetree

Fringetrees are small, deciduous trees or large shrubs with scaly winter buds. Leaves are opposite and large with entire leaf margins. Flowers are dioecious and showy. Fruit is a blue-black, single-seeded drupe.

Key to Species

I. Bundle scars are in a circular pattern. Side buds are globular with four to five pairs of bud scales. Leaves are borne mostly near the upper ends of the twigs. Leaves are generally oblong in shape and 3¼–8 inches (8½–20 cm) long. Foliage is dark green and shiny above and paler beneath. Flowers are dioecious, white, feathery, and borne in terminal panicles. The 4–8 inch (10–20 cm) long panicles open in May or June as the foliage begins to emerge. Fruit is dark blue and ripens in September on the female plants.

Chionanthus virginica—White Fringetree

Description of Species
White Fringetree—
Chionanthus virginica

A beautiful, large shrub or small tree, the white fringetree usually attains heights of 25–30 feet. Multiple stems are the rule. Fringetrees are planted for ornamental purposes. This small tree is native to southeastern Ohio in restricted areas. Fringetrees are most common in Scioto County, along rugged ravines and the lower slopes of larger streams.

Fringetrees are small, deciduous trees or large shrubs with scaly winter buds. Bundle scars are in a circular pattern. Side buds are globular with four to five pairs of bud scales. Branches are spreading, stout, and somewhat smooth with gray to greenish brown bark.

Leaves are opposite and large with entire leaf margins. Leaves are borne mostly near the upper ends of the twigs. Leaves are generally oblong in shape and 3¼–8 inches (8½–20 cm) long. Foliage is dark green and shiny above and paler beneath. The leaves are leathery to the touch. Fringetrees are likely to be the last plant to leaf out in the spring and are long-lived trees.

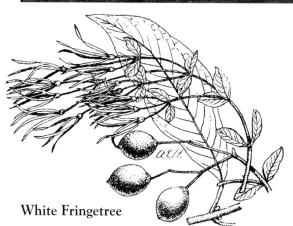

White Fringetree

196

Flowers are white and, when in full bloom, are strikingly attractive with drooping, fringed, or feathery blossoms. Flowers are dioecious and fragrant. Male flowers are said to be more attractive. The 4–8 inch (10–20 cm) long terminal panicles open in May or June as the foliage begins to emerge. Fruits are blue-black, single-seeded drupes and ripen in September on the female plants.

Paulownia — Paulownia

Paulownia is a medium-sized, deciduous tree with superposed, scaly buds. Leaves are opposite, entire, or shallowly lobed. Leaves may be somewhat toothed on young plants. Lavender flowers open in terminal panicles. The fruit is a two-valved capsule with numerous winged seeds.

Key to *Paulownia* Species

I. Leaves are simple and large, 4¾–10 inches (12–25 cm), and sometimes 20 inches (51 cm) long. Leaves are usually entire but are sometimes three-lobed on vigorous plants. Pith is chambered or sometimes hollow. Buds are normally superposed (one above another). Flowers are large, violet, and slightly fragrant. May or June flowers are followed by fruit in September to November.

Paulownia tomentosa—
Royal Paulownia (Empress Tree)

Description of Species
Royal Paulownia (Empress Tree)— *Paulownia tomentosa*

Paulownia is an introduced tree from China and Japan reaching 50 feet in height. This tree has escaped cultivation in few local areas of southern Ohio. In the Smokey Mountain National Park this tree has destroyed native vegetation on rocky sites such as cliff faces and is viewed as a serious weed. This is a danger that should be considered when introducing exotic species. This tree has proven to be quite urban-tolerant and is common in the inner cities of the south. It reseeds itself readily in disturbed urban sites where it is not winterkilled.

Leaves are simple, and large, 4¾–10 inches (12–25 cm), sometimes 20

Royal Paulownia (Empress Tree)

197

inches (51 cm) long. Leaves are usually entire but may be three-lobed on vigorous plants. Leaves are broad and heart-shaped, and they gradually taper to a point. The leaf base is cordate.

Buds are normally superposed (one above another). Twigs are olive brown in color, pubescent, stout, and heavily lenticeled. Pith is chambered or sometimes hollow. Catalpa has similar foliage but has continuous pith. Flower buds are borne in terminal panicles and are conspicuous through the winter. The flower buds make an excellent identification feature.

Flowers are purple and fragrant. Individual flowers are over an inch (25 mm) in diameter and are borne in terminal panicles that are a foot (30 cm) long. The flowers are carried against the foliage as a backdrop and are quite attractive in summer. The dark brown fruit is a two-valved, 1-inch (25 mm) diameter capsule with numerous winged seeds that mature in September to November. Fruit holds throughout the winter in 1 foot (30½ cm) long, upright panicles and is a good identification feature, as are the flower buds.

More recently, this tree has become a timber-crop plant and is being raised on plantations. This is one of the most valuable timber species in the United States despite the fact that the wood is not used in this country. It is the preferred wood for oriental lacquer ware. Population pressure prevents it from being grown in its former range. It is an excellent export crop for the United States. Ohio is the northern limit of its adaptability. In Ohio, paulownia winterkills easily unless cold-hardy seed sources are used. Even then the plant can be damaged in an unusually cold winter as happened in the Smokey Mountains a decade ago.

Catalpa — Catalpa

Catalpas are deciduous trees with scaly buds. Terminal buds are absent. Leaves are opposite or whorled and carried on long petioles. Leaf margins are entire. Flowers are borne in terminal panicles and are quite showy. Fruits are long, narrow, pod-like capsules, separating into winged seeds in the spring.

Key to *Catalpa* Species

I. Leaves are 6–12 inches (15–30½ cm) long with acuminate leaf tips. Foliage has no odor when crushed. Flowers are white with yellow-striped or brown-dotted throats. Flowers are borne in comparatively small terminal panicles. Flowers open in June.

Catalpa speciosa—Northern Catalpa

II. Leaves are 4–8 inches (10–20 cm) long with abruptly acuminate leaf tips. Foliage has an unpleasant odor when crushed. Flowers are white with yellow stripes and brown dots in the throat. Flowers are borne in many-flowered clusters and open in June and July.

Catalpa bignonioides—Southern Catalpa

Description of Species
Southern Catalpa—*Catalpa bignoniodes*

A small tree, not more than 20–40 feet high, the southern catalpa has widespreading branches that form an open head. The smaller size of the southern catalpa makes it desirable for small properties, but the litter is a concern in those situations. Often the southern catalpa was confused with the northern or hardy catalpa for reforestation purposes. Today neither catalpa is grown as a timber species.

Leaves are smaller than *Catalpa speciosa* and are only 4–8 inches (10–20 cm) long with abruptly acuminate leaf tips. Leaf attachment is opposite or whorled. Leaf bases are heart-shaped with entire leaf

Southern Catalpa

Southern Catalpa

margins. Foliage is light green and smooth above and hairy, or nearly so, beneath, especially along veins. Leaves have an unpleasant odor when crushed.

Terminal buds are absent. Catalpas have small, hemispherical buds. Leaf scars are circular and look like small volcanos. Twigs are stout, heavily lenticeled, and downy. The color is red to yellowish-brown. Pith is white and continuous.

Flowers are borne in many-flowered terminal panicles and are quite showy. Flowers are white with yellow stripes and brown dots in the throat and open in June and July. Flowers open about two weeks later than the northern catalpa. Fruits are 6–20 inches (15–51 cm) long with narrow, pod-like capsules separating into winged seed in the spring. Fruit is conspicuous through the winter and a positive identification feature for catalpa in Ohio. Fruit and flowers are a litter problem.

Northern Catalpa—*Catalpa speciosa*

The hardy catalpa was originally native from southwestern Indiana to southeastern Missouri and northeastern Arkansas. The hardy catalpa has been widely planted in Ohio for ornamental purposes. They are thrifty trees that develop straight trunks and reach 75 feet in the forest. These trees are very urban-tolerant. Litter from foliage, flowers, and fruit is a concern in landscape settings and falls throughout the year.

The simple leaves are opposite or whorled and carried on long petioles. Leaves are 6–12 inches (15–30½ cm) long and 4–5 inches (10–13 cm) wide. Leaves are heart-shaped at the base with acuminate leaf tips. Leaf margins are entire. The bruised leaves have no odor.

Catalpas have imbricate or scaly buds. Terminal buds are absent. The twigs are stout, smooth, yellowish-brown, and marked with large leaf scars. Leaf scars are circular and look like small volcanos. The buds are very small. Twigs are stout, heavily lenticeled, and downy. The color is red to yellowish-brown. Pith is white and continuous. The bark on old trees is fissured, ridged, and dark gray-brown.

Flowers are borne in erect, 8–10 inch (20–25 cm) high terminal panicles and are quite showy. Flowers are white with yellow-striped or brown-dotted throats and open in June. The lower lobe of the corolla is notched. Fruits are 12 inches (30½ cm) long with narrow, pod-like capsules separating into winged seeds in the spring. The fruit is conspicuous all winter and is a positive identification feature for catalpa in Ohio.

This species was formerly planted because of its rapid growth and durable wood. The wood is durable and light brown with a satiny surface and a kerosene-like odor. It is especially well-suited for fence posts and rails, as it lasts a long time in contact with the soil and does not require a preservative treatment. Insect damage has checked the growth of many plantations for use as fence posts.

Northern Catalpa

201

Viburnum — Viburnum

Viburnums are deciduous or evergreen shrubs or small trees, although Ohio's native viburnums are not evergreens. Winter buds are naked, valvate, or imbricate. Leaves are opposite with toothed, entire, or lobed margins. Flowers are small in umbel or panicle-like clusters. Fruits are drupes.

Key to Species

    I. Leaves are 1¼–3¼ inches (3–8½ cm) long. Petioles have narrow, not wavy, margins. Branches are rather rigid. Winter buds are short, pointed, red, and pubescent. Flowers are white and open in April or May. Fruits are blue-black, bloomy, and mature in September or October. This is a shrub or small tree growing 15–20 feet in height.

Viburnum prunifolium—Blackhaw Viburnum

Description of Species
Blackhaw Viburnum—*Viburnum prunifolium*

A small tree or shrub reaching 15–20 feet in height, the blackhaw viburnum has stiff, spreading branches that bear numerous, smooth, upright, slender twigs. It is an attractive ornamental shrub for landscaping and in bird sanctuaries. Blackhaw spreads readily by root suckers and is adapted to moist, fertile soils. This native plant is commonly available in the nursery industry.

Leaves are 1¼–3¼ inches (3–8½ cm) long. Ovate leaves have finely toothed leaf margins. Petioles have narrow, not wavy, margins. Winter floral buds are valvate, short, and pointed. Twigs are pubescent and have a red-brown covering or hairy bloom.

Flowers are borne in terminal clusters after the foliage is partially expanded. The white floral cluster is 2 inches (5 cm) across and attractive. Flowers open in April or May. Fruits are bluish-black and bloomy, and they mature in September or October. The edible fruit is sweet and was used for jams and jellies.

Blackhaw Viburnum

202

Glossary

A

Achene: A dry, indehiscent fruit such as that of dandelion.

Acuminate: Tapering at the end, long-pointed.

Acorn: The nut or fruit of an oak that is attached to the tree by a cap or saucer.

Acute: Sharp-pointed, ending in a point.

Adpressed: Closely and flatly pressed against something.

Aleopathic: Producing a chemical that has herbicidal properties and can reduce the growth of another plant.

Alternate: Leaves and leaf buds are borne alternating along the stem.

Anastomosing: Connecting by cross veins and forming a network. Reticulate.

Andro-dioecious: Staminate and bisexual flowers on different plants.

Anther: The pollen-bearing portion of the stamen.

Aril: An accessory covering on a seed usually attached where the seed is attached to the stalk. The covering is often fleshy.

Armed: Bearing spines or prickles.

Auriculate: Having an auricle or ear-shaped lobe at the base of a leaf or other organ.

Axil: The upper angle that a petiole or other organ makes with the axis that bears it.

Axis: The main or central line of development of a plant or organ.

Axillary: Situated in an axil.

B

Berry: A fruit in which the whole pericarp is fleshy or pulpy.

Bipinnate: Twice pinnate.

Bisexual: Having both stamens and pistils and also known as a perfect flower.

Blade: The expanded part of a leaf or petal.

Bract: Modified or reduced leaf subtending a flower or flower cluster.

C

Capsule: A dry dehiscent fruit of more than one carpel.

Catkin: A scaly, bracted spike of usually unisexual flowers.

Carpel: A portion of the pistil or ovary. Simple fruits have a single carpel but compound pistils have two or more united carpels.

Caudate: Bearing one or more taillike appendages, often on the apex of a leaf.

Chambered: (Pith) Hollow except for solid partitions.

Ciliate: Fringed with hairs.

Codominant: Said of two branches or axes of equal size.

Cordate: Heart-shaped.

Corymb: A flat-topped or convex flower cluster with the outer flowers opening first.

Crenate: Toothed with shallow, rounded teeth.

Crown: The top of a tree including the branches and foliage.

Cultivar: A cultivated variety that is often reproduced asexually.

Cuneate: Wedge-shaped.

Cutover: Harvested especially by clear cutting or removal of all trees on a site.

Cyme: A convex or flat flower cluster of the determinate type, the central flowers open first.

D

Deciduous: (Foliage) Leaves that are shed in the fall, not persistent.

Decurrent: Extending down the stem into other structures. The habit of an elm or oak tree is said to be decurrent.

Decussate: Alternating in pairs at right angles.

Dehiscent: Opening to emit its contents, as a capsule.

Dentate: Toothed with the teeth directed outward.

Diaphragm: A cross partition at the nodes of hollow or pithy stems. Also used to designate cross partitions at the internodes of pith stems.

Dioecious: Staminate and pistillate flowers on different plants.

Drupe: A fleshy, indehiscent fruit with a bony, usually one-seeded endocarp like a peach.

E

Ecotype: A subspecies or race especially adapted to an environment.

Elliptic: With the outline of an ellipse, about two times as long as broad.

203

Elongate: Drawn out or longer than wide.

Emarginate: With a shallow notch at the apex.

Endocarp: The inner layer of the pericarp.

Even pinnate: A compound leaf with leaflets opposite each other on the petioles but without a terminal leaflet resulting in an even number of leaflets.

Excurrent: Branches are in whorls with a strong central leader resulting in a pyramidal growth pattern. Spruce trees and many other conifers have excurrent branching patterns.

Exfoliate: To separate or peel off in flakes, scales, layers, or sheets.

Exocarp: The outer layer of the pericarp.

Exotic: Not native but introduced from another country.

F

Falcate: Sickle-shaped. Flat and curved, coming to a point.

Fetid: Having a foul odor such as decaying flesh.

Fissure: A crack or crevice in bark resulting from trunk expansion and growth.

Floral bud: A bud that contains only reproductive or floral initials.

Flower: The reproductive structure of a plant.

Foliate: Leaflike. Said of a bud in which you can see that the winter buds are modified leaves.

Follicle: A dry dehiscent fruit, a carpel opening only along one suture.

G

Germination: The initiation of growth by a seed or other resting body such as a spore.

Glabrous: Not hairy.

Glaucous: Covered with a bloom, usually bluish-white or bluish-gray.

Gland: A secreting body or appendage, but often includes gland-like bodies.

Globose: Rounded or spherical.

H

Head: A dense cluster or short spike of sessile or nearly sessile flowers.

Hydric: (Site) Moist or swampy.

I-K

Imbricate: Overlapping, as shingles on a roof.

Indehiscent: Not opening.

Inflorescence: A single flower or a group of flowers.

Internode: The portion of the stem between two nodes.

L

Lanceolate: Lance-shaped, about four times as long as broad, the broadest portion below or above the middle.

Lateral bud: Buds that give rise to lateral branches and are not at the end of the twig.

Leader: Main axis of a tree or plant.

Leaflet: Part (blade) of a compound leaf. Pinna.

Leaf blade: The expanded part of a leaf.

Leaf scar: The scar left when a leaf falls or is shed.

Lenticel: Breathing pores appearing as warty dots or patches on the surface of the stem.

Linear: Long and narrow with nearly parallel margins.

M

Mesic: (Site) A site that is intermediate in moisture such as the side of a hill.

Mesocarp: The middle layer of a pericarp.

Midrib: The central vein or rib of a leaf.

Mixed bud: A bud that contains both vegetative and floral initials.

Monoculture: A planting or grouping of plants of a single species.

Monoecious: With separate male and female flowers on the same plant.

Monopodial: Having growth and elongation continuing indefinitely, often without branching.

Mucilaginous: Secreting a sticky or mucus-like substance.

Mucronate: Tipped with a short abrupt point.

N

Node: The place on the stem which normally bears a leaf or leaves.

Nut: An indehiscent, one-seeded, hard and bony fruit.

O

Oblanceolate: Inversely lanceolate. Longer than wide and widest above the middle.

Oblique: Said of a leaf where the two sides of the leaf are unequal in size and slanted at the base.

Oblong: About three times as long as wide and with nearly parallel sides.

Obovate: Inversely ovate and wider above the middle.

Odd-pinnate: A compound leaf with leaflets opposite each other on the petioles and having a terminal leaflet resulting in an odd number of leaflets.

Opposite: Leaves and axillary buds are borne directly opposite one another on the stem.

Oval: Broad elliptic, about 1½ times as long as broad and rounded at the ends.

Ovary: The body which after fertilization becomes the seed.

Ovate: Egg-shaped and wider below the middle.

Ovoid: Egg-shaped.

P-Q

Palmate: Radiately lobed or divided with three or more veins arising from one point.

Palmately compound: A compound leaf with leaflets arranged like the fingers on your hand.

Panicle: A compound inflorescence of the racemose type with pedicled flowers.

Papilionaceous: Butterfly-like flowers. Found in legumes with pealike flowers.

Pedicel: The stalk of a flower or later the fruit.

Peduncle: The stalk of a flower cluster.

Peltate: Said of a leaf where the petiole is attached inside the leaf margin.

Perfect: (Flower) having both stamens (male organ) and pistil (female organ), bisexual.

Pericarp: The wall of the ripened ovary.

Petiole: The leaf stalk.

Petiolule: The stalk of a leaflet in a compound leaf.

Pinna: A single leaflet of a compound leaf. Pinnae is the plural of pinna.

Pinnate: Compound leaf with leaflets placed on each side of the rachis.

Pistil: The seed-bearing organ of the flower consisting of ovary, style, and stigma.

Pistillate: Bearing one or more pistils, female.

Pod: A dry fruit, like a bean pod that opens on one side.

Polygamous: Bearing unisexual and bisexual flowers on the same plant.

Pome: A fleshy fruit with a core like the apple.

Prickle: A weak, thorny projection arising from the epidermis or bark rather than the woody tissue.

Pruinose: Covered with a waxy covering or bloom.

Pseudo-terminal: A false terminal. A bud that arose from a lateral bud when the terminal portion of the twig died and was shed. The scar may be very small.

Pubescent: Covered with short, soft hairs.

R

Raceme: A single inflorescence of stalked flowers on a more or less elongated rachis. The flowers at the base of the floral cluster open first.

Racemose: Having flowers in racemes.

Rachis: An axis bearing flowers or leaflets.

Regular: (Flowers) with the parts of each whorl alike.

Reniform: Kidney-shaped.

Resinous: Bearing or covered in resin or sap.

Reticulate: Netted or net-like.

Root crown: The region where the trunk transitions into the main or transport roots.

Root flair: Root crown.

S

Samara: An indehiscent flattened fruit that is normally winged as in maple or elm.

Scabrous: Rough to the touch.

Schizocarp: A dry fruit that breaks into halves such as a maple.

Seed: A ripened ovule consisting of the embryo and its integuments.

Serrate: Toothed.

Sessile: Not stalked.

Sinuate: Wavy surface or margin but differing from undulate in that it is wavy in and out.

Sinus: The recess between the lobes.

Spatulate: Spoon-shaped with a rounded tip and an acuminate base.

Spike: A simple inflorescence with the flowers sessile or nearly so on a common axis.

Spine: A sharp, pointed outgrowth of a stem, leaf, or other organ containing vascular tissue. Another term for thorn.

Stalk: The nontechnical term for an elongate support structure such as a pedicle or peduncle.

Stamen: The pollen-bearing male organ of the flower.

Staminate: (Flowers) Male flowers bearing only functional stamens.

Stipule: An appendage at the base of the petiole, usually one on each side.

Stomata: Orifices in the epidermis of a leaf.

Stomatic: Bearing stomata.

Stomatiferous: See stomatic.

Stone: The hard, usually one-seeded, endocarp of a drupe.

Strobile: An inflorescence with imbricated scales or bracts. A cone.

Subtend: Enclosed in the axil.

Superposed: One above another.

Suture: A line of dehiscence or groove masking a union.

Sympodial: Having the elongation of a stem or axis periodically interrupted with the elongation of a lateral.

Syncarp: A fleshy, aggregate fruit.

T

Terminal bud: The bud that is at the terminus of the twig is sometimes called the primary bud.

Ternate: In threes.

Thorn: A sharp modified stem usually arising from woody tissue and containing vascular tissue. Another term for spine.

Tomentose: Covered with short, dense, hairs.

Truncate: Ending abruptly as if cut off. Flat.

U

Umbel: An inflorescence with pedicels or branches arising from the same point.

Undulate: Wavy surface or margin. Used here as wavy up and down.

Unisexual: An inflorescence with flower of a single sex.

V

Valvate: Meeting at the edges without overlapping.

Variety: A population of plants below species that have similar characteristics and are usually reproduced from seed.

Vegetative bud: A bud that contains only vegetative initials such as leaves.

Villous: Covered with long, soft, usually curved hair. Hair is not matted.

Viscid: Sticky.

W

Whorled: Leaves and axillary buds are borne three or more at one point on the stem.

Woolly: Covered with long, dense, and often matted hairs.

X

X: A notation used before the genus or species denoting an intergeneric or interspecific hybrid.

Xeric: (Site) A dry site such as the top of a ridge.

Index